A New Library of
the Supernatural

Minds Without Boundaries

Minds Without Boundaries

by Stuart Holroyd

Doubleday and Company, Inc.
Garden City, New York, 1976

EDITORIAL CONSULTANTS:

COLIN WILSON
DR. CHRISTOPHER EVANS

Series Coordinator: John Mason
Design Director: Günter Radtke
Picture Editor: Peter Cook
Editor: Eleanor Van Zandt
Copy Editor: Mitzi Bales
Research: Marian Pullen
General Consultant: Beppie Harrison

Library of Congress Cataloging in Publication Data

Holroyd, Stuart
Minds Without Boundaries
(A New Library of the Supernatural; v. 10)
1. Psychical Research I. Title II. Series
BF1031.H647 1976 133.8 75-34861
ISBN 0-385-11320-X

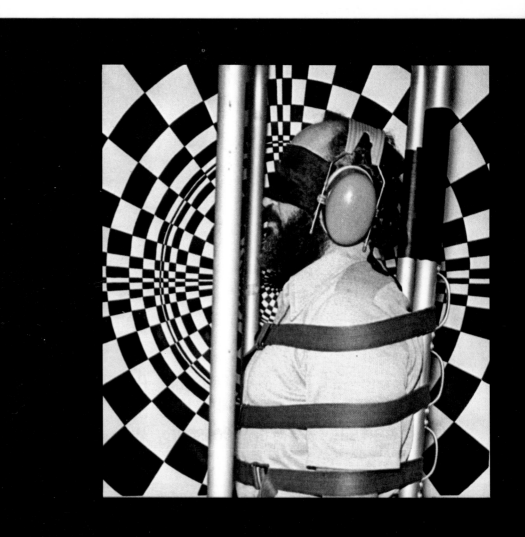

Doubleday and Company
ISBN: 0-385-11320-X

Library of Congress Catalog
Card No. 75-34861

A New Library of the Supernatural
ISBN: 11327-7

© 1976 Aldus Books Limited, London

Printed and bound in Italy by
Amilcare Pizzi S.p.A.
Cinisello Balsamo (Milano)

**Frontispiece: a test of extrasensory perception.
Above: testing the effects of sensory deprivation.**

Minds Without Boundaries

The idea that the human mind can transcend the five senses is not a new one, but the scientific exploration of that interesting idea is. Here is the story of how far modern investigations have come in the effort to explain psychic phenomena such as telepathy, clairvoyance, and psychokinesis.

Contents

1

In Search of the Unknown

It was the custom of Madame D., a French-woman, to take a bath every evening about six o'clock. One evening, shortly after getting into the tub, she began to feel ill. She didn't know that a leak in a gas pipe or an in-adequately closed valve had let gas escape into the bathroom. Mme. D. managed to press a call bell located near the tub just before she was overcome by the fumes and slid down into the water. An instant later, her husband rushed into the bathroom, pulled her out of the water, and restored her to consciousness.

After she was able to talk again, her husband asked her if she had experienced a

Unusual phenomena have always intrigued and fascinated us. Dreams that come true, the icy premonition that turns into the tragedy of tomorrow, the eerie sense of having been exactly here, doing exactly this, once before—all these are aspects of a kind of experience that has troubled peoples' minds and led them to find numerous explanations, ranging from magic to the effects of an overheated imagination. Right: an engraving of 1845 showing six hypnotized people getting a glimpse of their futures.

CLAIRVOYANCE.

"One of the more exciting discoveries of modern science"

fleeting vision of her past life in minute detail—as drowning people are said to. Mme. D. replied that she had seen a vision, but not the kind one would expect. Instead of seeing her husband and children and events from her past, she had seen the face of a casual acquaintance, Mme. J. "She was near me," said Mme. D., "looking at me sadly. It was impossible in those few moments to remove her from my eyes and thoughts."

The next morning, completely recovered, Mme. D. received word of the death of Mme. J. The woman had been drinking rather heavily on the previous evening, had gone into the bathroom to take a bath, and had drowned in the tub before she could call for help. The time: about six o'clock.

Was it sheer coincidence that at the moment of her near-tragedy Mme. D. should think of a woman she knew only slightly, who at the same time was undergoing a similar experience? A strictly rational view of this incident (adapted from René Warcollier's *Experiments in Telepathy*) would indicate a "yes" answer. Mme. D. had no way of knowing by normal means that the other woman's life was in danger at that moment. The persistent image of Mme. J. was simply—according to his viewpoint—a peculiar mental association, a trick of the mind with no causal relationship to Mme. J.'s crisis. In other words, a coincidence.

All of us experience odd coincidences at one time or another, even if they're not as dramatic as the vision of Mme. D. We may suddenly for no apparent reason think of a song that was popular perhaps 15 or 20 years ago, switch on the radio, and hear that particular song being played. Or we think of a friend, and a moment later that friend telephones.

Although we are sometimes tempted to think there may be a connection between the two events, most of us don't really believe in such a connection. Our everyday experience tells us that the only way we can get information is through our senses. We cannot know that the radio station is playing the song we thought of until we switch it on and hear it. We cannot know that the friend is dialing our number because we cannot hear or see the friend at that moment. On answering the phone we may say, "I must be psychic, I was just thinking of you!" But we don't seriously believe that our mind can, so to speak, bypass the senses and get information the senses cannot supply.

Increasingly, however, evidence is suggesting that it *is* possible for the mind to transcend the senses. Some of the evidence is startling, such as the experience of Mme. D. Some of it is somewhat unexciting, such as the ability to guess correctly more often than chance would allow which card will turn up next as one goes through the pack. Not all of the evidence is conclusive. But there is enough strong evidence to suggest that occasionally—perhaps frequently—direct mind-to-mind contact does take place. Today there are many scientists who would agree that some kind of mental link existed between Mme. D. and Mme. J. at the moment both were in danger. How such a link is established no one can say; but that it can be established is one of the more exciting discoveries of modern science.

Not only is mind-to-mind contact possible; but it also seems possible that some minds can get information from inanimate objects without using the senses. This apparently is something that the wife of the American novelist Upton Sinclair was able to do. Back in the 1920s, Mrs. Sinclair discovered that she could reproduce drawings in sealed envelopes, and in his book *Mental Radio* Sinclair tells the story of the discovery. Mrs. Sinclair had experienced a certain amount of pain from illnesses and had learned to exert mental control over this pain. She developed the ability to relax completely, to clear her mind of random thoughts, and to concentrate on a single idea. Her awakening interest in psychic powers developed further when the Sinclairs became acquainted with a young man named Jan, who performed an amazing variety of mental and physical feats including levitation. Mrs. Sinclair established a strong rapport with Jan, and was often able to describe in detail what he was doing at a given moment when he was far away from her. One day she jotted down a dream she had had about him, in which he brought her a little basket of flowers—pink roses and violets. She sketched the outline of the basket and flowers. The next day she received a letter from him. In it, through slits cut in the paper, he had inserted some violets and pink cosmos. The shape that the flowers made on the paper roughly followed the outline of the squat basket she had drawn.

Over the next year or two, Mrs. Sinclair did 290 drawings attempting to copy drawings made by her husband, his secretary, and her own brother-in-law. Some of her successful efforts are shown on pages 10–11. She occasionally wrote comments on her drawings to compensate for her limitations as an artist and to express more precisely the image in her mind's eye. Sometimes she simply wrote what she saw. In an early experiment her brother-in-law, who was in Pasadena some 40 miles away, drew a picture of a fork. At the same agreed-upon time, Mrs. Sinclair directed her powers of concentration toward his mind, and finally wrote: "See a table fork. Nothing else." In some cases, only part of the original drawing seemed to come through—for Sinclair's drawing of a steamboat she did only the smokestack with smoke coming out of it. Partial successes often resembled the shape of the original drawing—a pocket watch, for example, was seen as a wheel.

Out of the 290 drawings, the Sinclairs counted 65 as successes, 155 as partial successes, and the remaining 70 as failures. Acutely aware that most thoughtful people of his day regarded anything suggesting the occult with a certain amount of contempt, Sinclair went to great pains to stress his and his wife's commitment to a rational view of the world. His socialist friends were critical of this aberration on the part of one of their spokesmen, and one of them wrote a newspaper article entitled "Sinclair Goes Spooky." Sinclair answered their objections with all the eloquence he could command, stating: "I don't like to believe in telepathy, because I don't know what to make of it, and I don't know to what view of the universe it will lead me, and I would a whole lot rather give all my time to my muck-raking job . . . In short, there isn't a thing in the world that leads me to this act, except the conviction which has been forced upon me that telepathy is real, and that loyalty to

the nature of the universe makes it necessary for me to say so."

Today, nearly half a century after Sinclair wrote those words, the situation regarding the "spooky" has changed somewhat. If he were writing today, he would not need to be so defensive. Parapsychology—the branch of psychology dealing with telepathy and other psychic abilities—has established itself as a scientific discipline. In 1969 the Parapsychological Association, an international organization of parapsychologists, finally won membership in the American Association for the Advancement of Science. The parapsychologists' bid for membership was championed by the world-renowned anthropologist Margaret Mead. Her plea for their admission to the prestigious scientific body included these words: "The whole history of scientific advance is full of scientists investigating phenomena that the Establishment did not believe were there. I submit that we vote in favor of this association's work." The final vote was six to one in favor of admission.

The English magazine *New Scientist* found in a poll of its readers a few years ago that 70 percent of the respondents, mainly scientists and technicians, believed in the possibility of extrasensory perception. Of course, to believe in the possibility of something is not the same as believing in the thing itself. Even so, the high percentage suggests that the suspicious, if not hostile, attitude of scientists toward parapsychology is not as prevalent as it was in the past.

Mainstream science has impressive achievements to its credit, technological innovations that were inconceivable a

Above: Mary Craig Sinclair. Her telepathic powers inspired her husband, the crusading Socialist writer Upton Sinclair, to become an amateur psychical researcher with her as his subject. Over a period of three years he conducted experiments in which she read the minds of others to draw the same picture they had drawn. Participants in the experiments included her brother-in-law, Sinclair himself, and his secretary. Sinclair classified the many drawings as successes, partial successes, and failures. Success meant that her drawing had "some easily recognized element" of the original, even if it was only the outline. Her success rate was impressive. Right: this drawing of a man, labeled "man running can't draw it" bears a great similarity to Sinclair's man in movement.

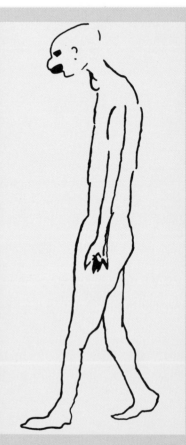

century ago and that have given us undreamed-of control over our environment and the forces of nature. But in spite of all the great changes it has effected in our environment, there are certain aspects of ourselves that mainstream science has not been able to make any sense of, aspects that not only fail to fit into its picture of reality but also actually challenge that picture. As the awareness grows that the human is a threatened species, and that our swift technological advance has disrupted delicate balances in nature that are essential to our survival, more and more people are opening their minds to alternatives to the scientific-rationalist view of the world. Cultures, philosophies, and religions that were formerly regarded as primitive and barbarous are being looked at with new interest. People are asking whether, in traveling so far so fast, we might not have left something behind. Might there not be something useful for us to learn both from neglected areas of the human psyche and from backward or primitive areas of the world?

In 1973 the Parapsychology Foundation of New York sponsored a conference in London on the theme "Parapsychology and Anthropology." The highlight of the conference was a paper entitled "African Apprenticeship" read by an Englishman named Adrian Boshier, who is also a witch doctor.

After years of living among the tribesmen of South Africa, Boshier had become accepted by them as a brother. Finally they invited him to undergo the 12 degrees of initiation that would qualify him as a witch doctor. Boshier's experiences have convinced him that the secrets and magical rites of the *sangomas*,

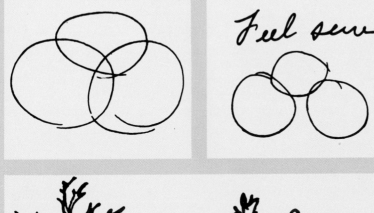

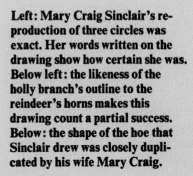

Left: Mary Craig Sinclair's reproduction of three circles was exact. Her words written on the drawing show how certain she was. Below left: the likeness of the holly branch's outline to the reindeer's horns makes this drawing count a partial success. Below: the shape of the hoe that Sinclair drew was closely duplicated by his wife Mary Craig.

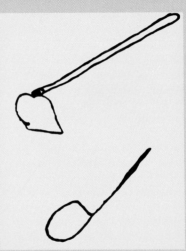

Above: a group photograph of the
1973 Conference on Parapsychology
and Anthropology held in London.
Adrian Boshier, an anthropologist
who had been initiated as a
witch doctor in South Africa, is
the first on the left, back row.

Right: an African diviner of
the kind who helpfully accepted
Boshier, reading his shells and
bones cast on the ground in
front of him. The skills of men
like these, dismissed by the
early European explorers as mere
superstition, have since been
recognized as being considerably
more effective and sophisticated
in their psychological element
than any explorer ever imagined.

as they call themselves, are not merely superstition. They are, in more colorful guise, the same kinds of phenomena studied in western parapsychology laboratories. The difference is that whereas in the West these phenomena are viewed with suspicion, the tribesmen Boshier knew accepted them as true.

In his paper for the London conference, Boshier gave several examples of the psychic powers of the sangomas. On one occasion he had narrowly escaped being attacked by a leopard while he was exploring an ancient copper mine. Later, on his way back to Johannesburg, he passed through a village in which lived an old woman sangoma whom he knew. He found her sitting in her "hut of the spirits," throwing the bones that she used as aids to divination. She became agitated, for she said she could make no sense of what the bones were telling her. "All I can see is the underworld, the underground," she said. Boshier told her about his exploration of the ancient mines, which put her mind at rest. But she warned him, "You must be very careful when you go down there, as the gods of the underworld can be very dangerous. Also, I see you here in my bones next to the leopard. The leopard, too, was in that place, and he does not like people in his home. You must be very careful of this animal—I see you were right next to him."

Tales of the psychic powers of witch doctors have been told by European travelers ever since Africa was opened up to trade and exploration in the 19th century. A typically strange story was told by a hunter and merchant named D. Leslie in a book privately published in Edinburgh in 1875.

Leslie had sent out his local elephant hunters with instructions to meet him on a certain date at a selected spot. They failed to turn up, so he consulted a local witch doctor who demanded to know the number of missing hunters and their names. He then made eight fires, one for each hunter, threw in some roots that produced a sickly smelling smoke, took some medicine, and fell into trance.

After about 10 minutes, he came out of the trance. He raked through the ashes of each of the fires in turn, and told Leslie what had happened to each of his hunters. One had died of fever and his gun was lost, another had been killed by an elephant but his gun had been recovered by another member of the party, a third had killed four elephants and was bringing back their tusks. The survivors, he said, would not be home for three months, and would travel by a different route than that previously chosen. Three months later, Leslie was able to confirm every detail of the witch doctor's account.

Of course, such stories do not prove anything. They are the testimonies of individuals not supported or confirmed by independent investigation, and we know very well that we cannot always trust the evidence of our senses or the reliability of our memory. We see and remember what we want to, often for reasons of which we are not aware. It may be argued that man's mind is avid for wonders, mysteries, and sensations, and is uncritical and easily deceived when it comes across them. Marvelous tales told by travelers have enthralled listeners in taverns, at firesides, and around campfires throughout human history. Today, tales that are equally marvelous, sensational,

The Witch Doctor Takes a Message

Father Trilles, a French missionary, became friends with a celebrated African witch doctor who told him one day that he was going to "a big palaver of all the magicians of this region." The meeting was the next day, but in a place that was four days' walk away. This made Father Trilles skeptical, so the witch doctor invited him to witness his departure.

Testing his friend, the missionary asked him to stop off in a village three days' walk distant and ask another friend to bring him some cartridges. The witch doctor agreed.

That night in his hut the witch doctor smeared a red liquid smelling of garlic all over his body. He chanted and made gestures during the process. Suddenly a large snake descended from the roof and wrapped itself around the witch doctor's body. He fell into a trancelike sleep, his body rigid and his lips flecked with foam. The snake disappeared.

Father Trilles stayed in the hut beside the witch doctor's motionless body all that night. The next morning the magician slowly returned to consciousness. He told his friend about the reunion, and said he had delivered the message.

Three days later Father Trilles' friend arrived with the cartridges.

and inexplicable enthrall readers of scientific books as well.

In a New York parapsychology laboratory in 1973 the artist and well-known psychic Ingo Swann underwent a number of tests, carefully observed by scientists and recorded by a television camera. In one test he sat in a chair in the middle of the room and tried to "see" the contents of a cardboard box suspended from the ceiling. No one present knew what was in the box, and the only way to see into it would have been to climb on a ladder. After concentrating for several minutes with his eyes closed, Swann sketched the shapes and identified the colors of the hidden objects. The test was repeated eight times, and each time he scored a hit. Explaining how he did it, Swann said that he went into trance, then felt his spirit float to the ceiling, look into the box, and return to his body. This claim the scientists could neither prove nor disprove, but their electronic equipment did record a noticeable change in his brainwave output before he drew each picture.

Other people have reported the experience of traveling out of the body, but their accounts—usually involving an illness or other crisis—have little value as evidence. The experiments with Ingo Swann illustrate how in the last few decades the study of the strange and unexplained faculties of the human mind has progressed from the anecdotal stage to the experimental. There are still, however, some critics of parapsychology who reject the experimental evidence and say that delusion, wishful thinking, and outright lying are as rife in the laboratory as in the tavern. Although scientific opinion is more favorable to parapsychology than it was 40 or 50 years ago, the psychic area is still clouded with emotion, distrust, and vagueness, and it is difficult for the layman to make sense of it all.

Parapsychology—or as it is sometimes called, psychical research—includes the study of several phenomena which are often referred to by the umbrella-term "psi" (pronounced "sigh"). These phenomena fall into two groups, mental and physical. The mental phenomena are covered by the term ESP (extrasensory perception), and include telepathy, clairvoyance, psychometry, precognition, and retrocognition. The physical phenomena include psychokinesis or PK (also called telekinesis) in its various forms including teleportation, levitation, and psychic healing; materialization and dematerialization; and out-of-the-body projection.

Telepathy is a word coined by the early psychical researcher F. W. H. Myers to denote the "transmission of thought independently of the recognized channels of sense." In an autobiographical book, *The Infinite Hive*, the English psychical researcher Rosalind Heywood gives a fascinating account of numerous telepathic experiences that occurred in her own life. She recalls an occasion in 1944 during World War II when her husband was due home on his first leave since the Normandy landings. His train from the Channel port of Folkestone was expected at 8 p.m. At 6:30 p.m. Mrs. Heywood lay down for a short rest after a hard day's work. She had been resting for 10 minutes when she got a compulsive urge to phone the station and check the time of the train. She learned that it would arrive an hour earlier than expected. She then got a

Above: the psychic Ingo Swann during a series of tests of his out-of-body vision. The experimenter Janet Mitchell is attaching electrodes to his scalp to monitor brain activity. A box containing the various target drawings was suspended about 10 feet over his head.

Right: drawings used during the Swann tests at the American Society for Psychical Research. Alongside are shown what Swann drew in trying to reproduce the originals by mind reading.

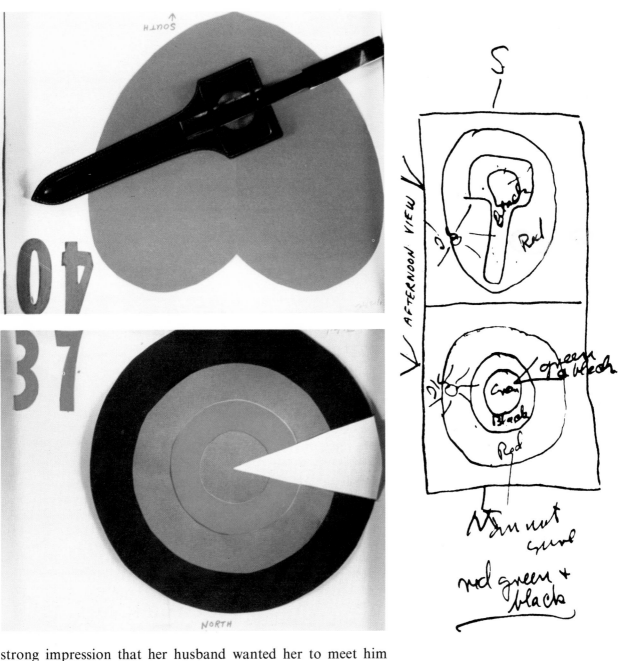

strong impression that her husband wanted her to meet him at the station and to have a porter ready. She just managed to reach the station and get a porter in time to meet her husband's train. He was delighted at his welcome, and he confirmed that during the journey from Folkestone he had deliberately tried to send her a mental message that the train would be early and he would need help. The telephone booths at Folkestone had had mile-long lines of people waiting for them, he explained, so he had decided to try telepathic communication instead.

Clairvoyance is the ability of a person to receive extrasensory knowledge of a thing or an event that is not known to any other human being at the time. If an experimenter in a parapsychology laboratory shuffles a deck of cards and gives the deck to the subject, and the subject succeeds in guessing the correct order of the cards in the shuffled deck, the feat may be called clairvoyant. Examples of pure clairvoyance are fairly rare, for usually some person—however distant—knows the information; and in such cases telepathy, not clairvoyance, is the likelier explanation. For example, the witch doctor who divined the fate of Leslie's hunters may have received the knowledge telepathically from one of the survivors. Similarly, Ingo Swann's discovery of the contents of the box may have been due neither to out-of-the-body projection nor to clairvoyance, but to telepathy with the absent person who placed the items in the box.

Psychometry, or object-reading, is a special kind of clairvoyance in which the subject receives information about a person extrasensorily by handling an object associated with that person. In his book *Supernormal Faculties in Man*, the French parapsychologist Eugène Osty described how the psychic Mme. Morel once traced a missing person. She was given a scarf from his wardrobe, but not told his name. After describing a forest, and giving its approximate location, she focused on the body that she saw lying on the ground there, and said: "He is bald, has a long nose . . . a little white hair above his ears and at the back of his head . . . wearing a long coat . . . soft shirt . . . hands closed . . . I see one finger which has been hurt . . . very old and wrinkled . . . pendant lips . . . Forehead much furrowed, very high and open . . . He is lying on his right side, one leg bent under him. . . ." The search team found the man's body lying where she had said it was, in exactly that position.

Precognition and **retrocognition** are the terms for paranormal knowledge of future and past events respectively. There are many puzzling accounts of precognition on record. In 1956 the American psychic Jeane Dixon wrote in a magazine article: "the 1960 election will be won by a Democrat, but he will be assassinated or die in office." A few weeks before President Kennedy's assassination in Dallas she told a friend who was close to the Kennedys, "The President has just made a decision to go someplace in the South that will be fatal for him. You must get word to him not to make the trip."

Retrocognition is less frequently reported, for it is obviously more difficult to distinguish paranormal knowledge of the past from normal knowledge. The classic case is that of two English women, Miss Moberly and Miss Jourdain. On a visit to the Palace of Versailles on a summer afternoon in 1901, they found (or imagined) themselves thrown back in time to the 18th century, and saw the costumed courtiers and all the paths and buildings as they had been in the days of Marie Antoinette. Fifty years later in 1951 two other Englishwomen visiting Dieppe on the coast of Normandy woke in the middle of the night to sounds of battle. Nothing was visible from their hotel window, but they distinctly heard the sound of gunfire coming from the direction of the beach, tanks rumbling along the roads, and aircraft zooming overhead. Later it was discovered that the occasion was precisely the ninth anniversary of the 1942 Dieppe Raid by Allied Forces, and that the women's account of their experience corresponded exactly with the time schedule of the actual invasion.

Above: Rosalind Heywood as both researcher and practitioner has been involved in various psi fields, most notably telepathy. She is a leading figure in psychical research in Britain.

Below: the medium David Young shown during an experiment on psychometry. He is attempting to give information about an early 19th-century pistol. He "felt a connection" with the letters WE—West—and a place name "possibly Brighton." In fact, the gun had originally been owned by a man named West, who joined the army in Brighton.

Psychokinesis is the movement of objects by mental energy or the power of "mind over matter." A California man recounts how, two nights after his wife's death, he had a strong sensation that she was present in the room, so he said: "If you are here and can hear me, give me a sign." He had no sooner spoken the words than a heavy model chariot with two horses crashed to the floor from a mantelpiece where it had stood for 12 years. Whether the power that moved it came from his wife's spirit, from the man himself, or from a natural cause is arguable, but the accumulated evidence on such phenomena—including clocks stopping or starting for no apparent reason, pictures falling from walls, and vases being hurled across rooms—testifies to the reality of psychokinesis.

Above: famous clairvoyant Jeane Dixon with her crystal ball, which she uses for her feats of precognition. She predicted the death of Mahatma Ghandi and foresaw the Kennedy assassination. Left: the phenomenon of retrocognition, or being thrown back in time, is rare. One famous case, reconstructed in this photograph, involved two Englishwomen who visited the French palace of Versailles in 1901. They found themselves walking in the palace as it was some 200 years before with uniformed gardeners, costumed courtiers, and all the buildings as they had been in the 18th century. Below: in a Soviet experiment of psychokinesis, a psychic is apparently making a small ball rise up into midair.

Teleportation—less well authenticated than the kinds of phenomena mentioned above—is the ability to move an object from one place to another by psychic means. Andrija Puharich, a scientist who conducted a long series of experiments with the Israeli psychic Uri Geller, claims that on one occasion Geller teleported to Israel a camera case that Puharich had left in his home near New York, and that he had said he needed.

Levitation is the ability to rise from the ground or to raise material objects by paranormal means. Tales of levitations by saints or mystics are found in the literature of religions the world over. They are also common in the records of seances with 19th-century mediums. The most famous, controversial, and spectacular case was that performed by the British medium Daniel Dunglas Home, usually referred to as D.D. In front of several distinguished witnesses Home levitated, floated out of a third-story window, and reentered the building through the window of another room.

Psychic healing has a long history and includes some of the miracle cures performed by Christ and many of the Christian

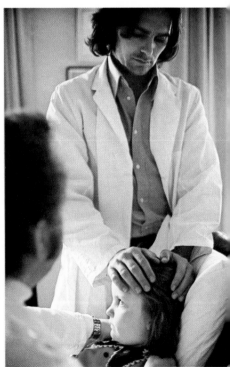

Left: the British medium Colin Evans, apparently successfully levitating during a public seance in London's Conway Hall in 1938.

Below: a student of the faith healer Ron Eager, working with Eager to heal a young child by the power of laying on of hands.

saints. Today psychic healing, or faith healing, is practiced not only by members of the clergy in the form of laying-on-of-hands, but also by people who, without representing any religious viewpoint, seem to be able to will a person to health. A different aspect of the same apparent power has been demonstrated in controlled experiments with plants, in which those plants that had prayers said over them developed into noticeably healthier specimens than the control group over which no prayers were said.

A bizarre variant of psychic healing is psychic surgery. In recent years many Europeans and Americans in terminal stages of illness have been going to the Philippines and Brazil and returning home to tell incredulous friends and doctors how local healers have apparently removed tumors from their bodies simply by massaging and kneading the flesh with their bare hands. Although some observers have been convinced that removal of tissue actually takes place in these treatments, others maintain that the operation is simply a conjuring trick.

Materialization, like psychic surgery, is a highly controversial phenomenon, and most psychical researchers would deny that it actually occurs. As the name implies, it involves the creation of material objects—sometimes living organisms—apparently out of nothing, or out of a substance called ectoplasm that exudes from a medium's body. Dematerialization is the reverse process, the causing of the materialized objects to disappear. One extraordinary story of materialization involved a seal. A zoologist named Mr. Bolton had cared for and prolonged the life of a large seal that had been harpooned, but in spite of his efforts, it had finally died. Ten days after the seal's death Bolton was at a Spiritualist seance when the medium cried out from her cabinet, "Take this great brute away, it is suffocating me." A seal emerged from the cabinet, waddled and flopped across the room, remained beside Bolton for a few moments, then returned to the cabinet and dematerialized. "There is no doubt in my mind," Bolton solemnly told a meeting of the London Spiritualist Alliance, "that it was the identical seal."

Out-of-the-body projection may be involuntary or deliberate. The files of doctors and psychiatrists the world over contain accounts of people who have had the alarming experience of being literally outside themselves and clearly seeing their own bodies objectively at a distance. Deliberate out-of-the-body projection, or astral travel, is a phenomenon well documented in the early records of many cultures.

These, then, are the phenomena, the strange powers and experiences that are collectively known as psi. Records attesting to the reality of psychic phenomena come from all ages and places, and from people of acknowledged intelligence and integrity. Yet argument about psi still rages, for the subject arouses people's hopes, fears, and prejudices. Perhaps more than any other question it sharply separates two distinct human types: those who believe that the universe is governed by rational and discoverable principles and who abhor the supernatural, and those who believe that anything is possible, that man has great powers as yet undeveloped, and that manifestations of the supernatural are glimpses of a superior and

Below: an engraving of 1887 of the medium Florence Cook with her famous materialization, Katie King. Florence Cook was closely studied by Sir William Crookes, an early psychical researcher. He claimed to have authenticated her powers, but there is still considerable speculation about his objectivity.

Right: a researcher, Professor A. J. Ellison, attempts to record the out-of-body experience of a hypnotized subject. Professor Ellison measures her electrical skin resistance, and carefully tests the depth of her trance.

Below: Ingo Swann in front of his painting *Aft Ship's View of Sagittarius* completed after what he claims was an out-of-body voyage into outer space. Swann apparently trained himself to leave his body at will. He is under conscious control and is fully awake during experiments on the nature of his abilities.

more exciting plane of reality than the one on which we normally live. Between the extremes of those who write off psi as rubbish and those who are ready to believe anything provided it confounds reason and science, are the majority of people. This majority takes a cautiously open-minded view. They think there must be something in it, are prepared to believe some things but not others, and are intrigued but rather bewildered by the whole subject.

There is one thing that can be said without raising anyone's temperature, however. It is that *psi occurs*. It's not a very exciting statement, but it gives us something to build on if we want to take a clear look at the subject and make some sense of it. Psi is useful not only because it is an umbrella term but also because it is a neutral one. To say that extrasensory perception occurs is more controversial, for it raises the question of how we know that the perceptions are *extra* and not simply a heightened degree of normal sensory perception. Most of the other terms—such as clairvoyance, telepathy, and materialization—have similar pitfalls. To say that psi occurs is simply to say that there are mental and physical events that in the present state of our knowledge cannot be explained.

"Our knowledge" in this context means the knowledge that modern, mainly Western, culture and science are founded on. Psi phenomena can easily be explained as the work of spirits or occult forces associated with gods, demons, or the planets, but to accept such explanations seems to the modern mind a retreat from reason back into the dark ages of superstition. This is the problem. Not only is psi inexplicable in terms acceptable to the modern mind, but it also appears to undermine certain concepts that are absolutely fundamental in our civilization—notably our ideas of time, causality, energy, mind, and matter. This is where attitudes enter the picture. Some people are completely happy with the Western worldview, and with its scientific and technological civilization. Others would like to see it changed for something less materialistic and more spiritual.

In this situation perhaps the first question we should ask is: What is important about psi? If we accept that it occurs, should we go on and ask how, why, and when it occurs, and risk undermining some of our most cherished and useful ideas and attitudes? Or should we consider it a mildly interesting curiosity and aberration?

The possibility that all humans may have some degree of psychic ability is one of the most exciting implications of parapsychology. Perhaps the limitations or boundaries of our minds are not real boundaries at all, but artificial ones of our own making. If these boundaries can be transcended, if psi faculties can be developed and trained, the implications for our society are profound. There is a growing feeling in the Western world today that some fundamental changes are essential if civilization is to survive. Many people believe that psi is important because it points the direction those changes might take. In the words of astronaut Edgar Mitchell, "survival seems to depend more than anything on a transformation of consciousness, an evolution of the mind."

The Colonel Takes Leave of his Body

Few people have had the strange experience of seeing their own body from outside it. One man who did is a British Army colonel. It happened when he was desperately ill with pneumonia. Through the haze of his illness he heard his doctor say there was nothing more that could be done. The colonel, however, promised himself, "You *shall* get better." He then felt his body getting heavier and heavier, and suddenly discovered he was sitting on top of the cupboard in the corner of the room. He was watching a nurse tending his own unshaven, apparently unconscious body. The colonel was aware of all the small details of the room. He saw the mirror on the dressing table, the frame of the bed, and his inert body under the bedclothes.

The next thing he remembers he was back in his body, and the nurse was holding his hand and murmuring, "The crisis has passed."

During his convalescence he told the nurse what had happened to him, describing the exact motions she had made and the details of the room that had been so clear to him. She suggested that perhaps he had been delirious.

The colonel had a different answer. "I was dead for that time," he said.

Early Psychical Research

The first recorded psychical researcher was King Croesus of Lydia, who lived in the 6th century B.C. In order to test which of a group of Greek and Egyptian oracles was the most skilled, he sent emissaries to each of them with instructions to ask them at a pre-arranged time: "What is King Croesus, the son of Alyattes, doing now?" He contrived something theoretically impossible to guess. He cut a lamb and a tortoise into pieces and cooked them together in a brass cauldron. In a brilliant feat of clairvoyance, the oracle at Delphi got the answer right.

Of course, King Croesus wasn't research-ing in the interests of science. He already

Literature is rich in tales of psychic experience, and in some cases—like that of Mary Shelley who dreamed the terrifying tale of Frankenstein—it has been the inspiration for literature. Right: Charles Dickens was another noted author who calmly admitted that many of his compli-cated plots and vivid characters first came to him in dreams.

"Modern psychical research has focused on... the mysteries of the mind"

believed in the supernatural powers of the oracles, and simply wanted to find out which of them was the best so that he could engage a reliable adviser. He chose well, for in time the clairvoyant and precognitive achievements of the Delphic Oracle became legendary. Her fondness for riddles and ambiguities, however, undermined her usefulness as a royal adviser, as King Croesus found to his cost. When she predicted that one of his campaigns would end in the destruction of a great army he went off to war with buoyant confidence, not dreaming that the doomed army was his own.

So long as people believed in the supernatural as a part of life there was no chance for scientific psychical research to get off the ground. That such a belief was prevalent in Shakespeare's day is obvious from his plays, in which the supernatural is often the pivot of the drama. In *A Midsummer Night's Dream*, for example, supernatural beings interact with mortals, weaving an intricate web of romantic complications. Shakespeare's audiences accepted the witches in *Macbeth* and the ghost in *Hamlet* at their face value. Modern audiences accept them in the context of the play but regard them as remnants of an age of superstition. A parapsychologist, engaged in studying unusual kinds of perception, might take a different view and ask questions that the Elizabethans could never have conceived. For example, when the witches greet Macbeth as "king hereafter," is this a precognition on their part, or are they picking up telepathically from Macbeth a wish that he would like to see fulfilled? When the ghost of Hamlet's father relates the circumstances of his death, is the whole incident perhaps an hallucinatory glimpse of the past on Hamlet's part? Such questions indicate some of the areas of concern of modern psychical research. It has not demystified the universe, but has focused attention on a different set of mysteries from those that preoccupied earlier ages: the mysteries of the mind.

Two conditions were necessary for the start of scientific psychical research: a society generally skeptical of all things supernatural, and a group of dedicated and intelligent scientists concerned about the limitations of such skepticism. It was not until the mid-19th century that these two conditions were fulfilled. The 18th century was skeptical enough, but it didn't produce the right people. Perhaps this was because reason had so recently been enthroned as a sovereign principle of knowledge. Few intellectuals of the Age of Reason would have risked ridicule by seriously examining the discredited beliefs of their superstitious forebears. When reason as an ideal gave way to romanticism with its emphasis on subjective experience, conditions became more favorable for the development of psychical research.

The poet Shelley, one of the major figures of the romantic age, was a morbid dreamer. In one dream he saw Lord Byron's dead daughter Allegra rise from the Gulf of Spezia, clasp her hands, and smile at him. In another he saw his friends Edward and Jane Williams die horribly in a house flooded by the sea. Not long after these nightmares, Shelley and Edward Williams died together off the coast of Italy, drowned in the Gulf of Spezia.

The great German poet Goethe reported a less ominous pre-

Above: a 19th-century view of the Delphic Oracle. A well-documented, classic example of a seer, the Oracle was consulted by many rulers. Her ambiguous utterances were interpreted by attendant priests.

Left: the three witches in *Macbeth* exemplify Shakespeare's use of psychic material. Curiously, *Macbeth* has come to be known among actors as an unlucky play. The superstition goes that the witches' incantations over their brew are in fact genuine black magic spells.

cognitive experience in his autobiography. One day he was riding on horseback along a footpath when he saw his own image riding toward him in the opposite direction, dressed in a suit such as he had never worn. He shook himself out of his reverie, and the vision vanished—but eight years later when he was again riding along the same path he suddenly realized that he was wearing exactly the suit that he had formerly dreamed of.

The novelist Charles Dickens also experienced a precognitive vision. He fell asleep in his office one evening and dreamed that he saw a lady in a red shawl standing with her back toward him. He didn't recognize her when she turned around, but she introduced herself as Miss Napier. He could make no sense of it, for he had never heard of any Miss Napier. But the following evening some friends visited him. They brought with them a stranger, a lady wearing a red shawl whom they introduced to him as Miss Napier.

In spite of his own psychic experiences and his frequent use of clairvoyant dreams and spirit manifestations in his novels, Dickens was strongly antagonistic to the craze for communication with the spirit world that swept through America and England in the middle of the 19th century. Perhaps when he heard of the "spirit rappings" in Hydesville, New York that launched the Spiritualist movement in 1848, he may have remembered how a great English writer of the previous century had been ridiculed for his interest in a similar phenomenon. In 1762 Dr. Samuel Johnson visited a house in Cock Lane, London where the ghost of a Mrs. Kent was said to be communicating by means of rappings that would occur only in the presence of the 12-year-old daughter of the house, Elizabeth Parsons. The ghost, which soon became famous throughout London, accused Mr. Kent of poisoning his wife. After Dr. Johnson had written a report on the ghost for a magazine, another investigator discovered that the rappings were produced by the girl Elizabeth, whose father was trying to blackmail Kent. Johnson and the other eminent people who had taken an interest in the affair were left looking rather foolish.

The Cock Lane Ghost affair was an inept attempt at an art that became highly skilled and sophisticated in the second half of the 19th century: the fraudulent production of allegedly spiritual phenomena. This was the age of the great physical mediums, nearly all of whom, with the exception of the greatest of them, D. D. Home, were at one time or another exposed in fraud. With fraudulent mediums producing rappings, spirit photographs, materialized spirit forms (always in semidarkness), automatic writing, and voices from the beyond that conveyed mundane and sentimental messages for a credulous public, it is not surprising that most serious and intelligent people should find the whole psychic business tasteless, tawdry, and repugnant. The characteristic attitude of the intellectuals was well expressed

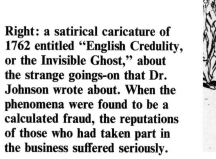

Above: the London house where mysterious rappings were reported by Samuel Johnson in 1762.

Right: a satirical caricature of 1762 entitled "English Credulity, or the Invisible Ghost," about the strange goings-on that Dr. Johnson wrote about. When the phenomena were found to be a calculated fraud, the reputations of those who had taken part in the business suffered seriously.

by the philosopher Thomas Henry Huxley in a letter declining an invitation to investigate Spiritualistic phenomena: " . . . supposing the phenoman to be genuine—they do not interest me. If anybody would endow me with the faculty of listening to the chatter of old women and curates in the nearest cathedral town, I should decline the privilege having better things to do. And if the folk in the spiritual world do not talk more wisely and sensibly than their friends report them to do, I put them in the same category. The only good that I can see in a demonstration of the truth of 'Spiritualism' is to furnish an additional argument against suicide. Better live a crossing-sweeper than die and be made to talk twaddle by a 'medium' hired at a guinea a seance."

But there were some highly intellectual and talented men who

Below: a watercolor showing a spectacular levitation, done in 1783. Even in a rational and scientific period, the belief in the possibility of paranormal behavior—like the floating nightshirted gentleman shown—persisted among many people.

Left: the Fox sisters levitating a table. Although their first communication with the spirits was simply by means of knocks and rappings inside their own house in Hydesville, New York—which had also been experienced by previous tenants—the scope of the phenomena widened when the sisters began to communicate with spirits outside their home.

Right: Daniel Dunglas Home was the greatest physical medium of his time. He produced materializations, psychokinetic effects, bodily elongation, and levitation. He was the only medium of the period never to have been detected in fraud while producing his spectacular effects, in spite of intensive investigation by many eminent psychical researchers.

didn't take Huxley's attitude, who thought that among all the dross there might just be the occasional nugget of solid gold, of significant new knowledge. Among them were Henry Sidgwick, F. W. H. Myers, and Edmund Gurney. These three men, all Fellows of Trinity College, Cambridge, and all sons of clergymen, were the founding fathers of systematic psychical research. Their individual, distinctive talents and personalities complemented each other and meshed together in a way that made them an ideal team for the investigative and theoretical work to which they devoted the greater part of their lives.

That they were the sons of clergymen is significant because undoubtedly a part of their motivation in pursuing psychical research was the hope of finding some grounds for reviving their religious faith, which had been undermined by the prevailing skeptical philosophy of the day. This is made clear by Myers in this famous passage in which he tells how he first broached the subject to Sidgwick: "In a star-light walk which I shall not forget I asked him, almost with trembling, whether he thought that when Tradition, Intuition, Metaphysic, had failed to solve the riddle of the Universe, there was still a chance that from any actual observable phenomena—ghosts, spirits, whatsoever there might be—some valid knowledge might be drawn as to a World

Right: a German drawing of a seance of the 1920s. These sessions, generally held with a medium, were conducted in dim light or total darkness to create what was said to be a suitable atmosphere for spirits. It also provided a suitable atmosphere for sleight-of-hand and other fraud.

Unseen. Already, it seemed, he had thought that this was possible; steadily, though in no sanguine fashion, he indicated some last grounds for hope; and from that night onwards I resolved to pursue this quest, if it might be, at his side."

Sidgwick, who in 1883 became professor of Moral Philosophy at Cambridge, possessed as sharp and critical an intellect as any person of his day. Myers' distinction was as a classicist, and he was qualified as a musician and a doctor as well. When Myers, Gurney, Sidgwick, and some other Cambridge and Oxford scholars founded the Society for Psychical Research in 1882, Sidgwick became its President and Gurney its Secretary, a job to which he subsequently devoted all his time and in which he did prodigious work. Myers also worked tirelessly as general organizer of the SPR, lecturing, writing, investigating and collecting material for its publications. Another early member of the SPR was Eleanor Sidgwick, wife of Henry Sidgwick and a prominent psychical investigator. Scientifically trained, she conducted some of the most important research done by the Society and, like her husband, served as its President.

The declared aim of the SPR was to "investigate that large body of debatable phenomena designated by such terms as mesmeric, psychical, and spiritualistic," and to do so "without prejudice or prepossession of any kind, and in the same spirit of exact and unimpassioned enquiry which has enabled Science to solve so many problems, once not less obscure nor less hotly debated." Like most intellectuals of their day, the founders of the SPR shared a belief that science was capable of solving virtually any mystery known to man.

Though the marvels performed by professional mediums were on the whole to be distrusted, Myers and Gurney became convinced that they must sometimes be genuine. This belief arose as a result of their investigation of William Stainton Moses, a

retired clergyman, an Oxford University degree holder, and, in Myers' words, a man of "manifest sanity and probity" who could not for a moment be suspected of fraud.

The records of the psychic effects produced by Stainton Moses are as sensational and as puzzling as those of the better known D. D. Home. Their authenticity is buttressed by the fact that before Moses discovered his own powers he distrusted Spiritualism, and is on record as having said of a book about Home that it was the dreariest twaddle he had ever come across. He began to have second thoughts when through a medium he received a strikingly accurate description of the spirit presence of a friend of his who had died. A few months after this occurrence he had his first experience of levitation. From then on, over a period of nine years, Moses experienced and apparently produced phenomena of the most extraordinary and occasionally alarming nature.

Sergeant Cox, a friend of Moses', wrote an account of a curious happening at his own home in June 1873. He and Moses were in the dining room passing half an hour before going out to a dinner party. Cox was opening letters and Moses was reading *The Times* when suddenly, frequent and loud rapping noises came from the dining table. The table was a large mahogany one that could barely be moved by the strenuous efforts of two men. But it began to sway to and fro, and then it moved several inches across the floor. Cox, a keen psychical researcher, realized that this was an invaluable opportunity to conduct some experiments. At his suggestion he and Moses stood two feet away from the table on opposite sides and held their hands about eight inches above it. After they had been waiting about a minute, the table rocked violently, moved seven inches along the floor, and tilted first toward one man and then toward the other. Finally Moses held his hands four inches above the end of the table and asked that it rise and touch his hand three times, which it promptly did.

What is notable in this account is that the noises and movements began unexpectedly, and were almost certainly not deliberately produced by Moses. The same is true of all the other strange things that happened to and around him. Once he found himself suddenly levitated, thrown down on his back on the table, then lifted up again and deposited on the sofa, all of which happened without his being in any way hurt. Frequently small objects from different parts of the house appeared over Moses' head and fell on the table in front of him, having apparently passed through walls or closed doors. When Moses held a seance his sitters could expect to be caressed by breezes heavy with perfumes, entertained by a variety of musical sounds—although there were no instruments in the room, and illuminated by psychic lights emanating from the floor. Materializations of hands and weaving columns of light that suggested human forms would appear in the room. An evening with Stainton Moses couldn't have been dull, and the wonders must have been enhanced by the thought that such a solemn and august gentlemen—free of any financial motive—would be unlikely to stoop to the low dodges of many a professional medium's elaborately rigged seance room.

Moses claimed that the remarkable physical phenomena that occurred in his presence were produced by spirits to prove the

authenticity of messages that they were communicating to the world through him by means of automatic writing. He published these spirit communications in 1883 as *Spirit Teachings*, a book that became the bible of Spiritualism.

Though Myers had no doubts about the integrity of Moses, he was skeptical about the alleged spirit intelligences and thought that there might be some other explanation for both the automatic writing and the physical phenomena. Unfortunately, by the time the Society for Psychical Research was formed, Moses' psychic powers had declined. He could not be studied under the controlled conditions that the Society sought to bring to all its investigations.

Though psychical phenomena were generally accepted at the time—by those who believed them—as proof of the existence of spirits, and therefore of the reality of survival after death, the founders of the SPR were well aware that this was really only an hypothesis. However much they may have personally longed to have their religious doubts allayed and to establish some definite proof of personal survival, they tried not to let this longing introduce a bias into their systematic investigative work. This work mainly involved conducting experiments in telepathy and clairvoyance, and collecting anecdotal evidence of these phenomena.

A public appeal for evidence got a substantial response and deluged Gurney and Myers with work. One of the respondents was a Manchester clergyman named Creery who had for some time been conducting experiments in telepathy with his five daughters. The Creerys became the first subjects of systematic and controlled research into telepathy conducted by the SPR.

The Creery family reproduced their successes before an investigating committee of the SPR under strictly controlled conditions. However, it was later discovered that the girls had cheated in some less tightly controlled experiments, and Myers and Gurney had to discount the impressive evidence for telepathy gathered in their own work with the Creerys.

In 1883, the year following the Creery experiments, Liverpool businessman Malcolm Guthrie discovered that some of his employees had been experimenting with thought-transference in their spare time, and had obtained remarkable results in transmitting simple drawings. His interest was aroused, so he and a friend, James Birchall, conducted their own experiments with two of the employees, Miss Relph and Miss Edwards, who were said to have shown exceptional ability. These experiments were so successful that they informed the SPR. Edmund Gurney went to Liverpool to supervise some tests himself.

The procedure varied slightly. Normally, the person chosen to do the drawing would do so in another room. The *percipient*—that is, the person who sees in a paranormal way—would be blindfolded and would sit opposite the agent, who would hold the drawing in such a way that the percipient could not have seen it even without the blindfold. The agent would stare intently at the drawing and concentrate on it until the percipient said she was ready to attempt to reproduce it, and her blindfold was removed. The period of concentration might last from half a minute to two or three minutes.

Above: William Stainton Moses, clergyman and medium. He began his psychic career as one of the earliest automatic writers, but increased his psychic range to include phenomena like rappings, levitation, and psychokinesis. Unfortunately, his gifts had subsided by the time he helped to found the SPR, and he was never tested under scientific controls. Below: table rapping became the first popular method of spirit communication, with hundreds of domestic seances like this one.

Many of the attempts were failures. In other cases parts of the diagram would be inverted, or transformed in some other way. A vertical line flanked by two circles was interpreted as a pair of scissors. The number of partial or complete successes was strikingly high, many times higher than could be attributed to chance. In one series of trials, reproduced on pages 38–39, all six attempts were either wholly or partially successful.

The Professor of Physics at Liverpool University at this time was young Oliver Lodge, later knighted for his discoveries in the fields of electricity and radio. He heard about the Guthrie experiments and supervised a new series of tests with the young women, introducing some variations of his own and bringing to the work the care and thoroughness that distinguished his work as a research physicist. In one of his variations he had two agents concentrating on different shapes, a square and a cross. The subject, who was used to receiving telepathic transmission from one agent only and didn't know that two were being used in this case, was at first confused but finally drew a cross within a square. The plausible inference seemed to be that the subject had received both messages and assumed, consciously or subconciously, that they formed a single image.

In addition to their experimental work, the indefatigable Gurney and Myers investigated numerous reported cases of spontaneous telepathic and clairvoyant experiences. Advertisements in *The Times* and other periodicals brought the reports flooding in. In 1883 they wrote 10,000 letters between them, and conducted hundreds of interviews. To help with the work they enlisted an Oxford scholar, Frank Podmore, whose skepticism and thoroughness in investigation were an invaluable contribution.

As they sifted and analyzed the many reports, the researchers noticed that the largest single category was of what they called "crisis apparitions." In these cases, a person had experienced a vivid, often very realistic, hallucination of another person at a moment later found to coincide with a moment of crisis in that other person's life. The crisis was usually the person's death, or serious injury or illness. In some cases the hallucination was auditory rather than visual: the person's voice would be heard at the time of his crisis.

After three years of research, Gurney, Myers, and Podmore published their evidence for telepathy, both spontaneous and experimental, in the form of a large book entitled *Phantasms of the Living*. This book, the first major work published by the SPR, contained reports of 702 cases of spontaneous psychic experiences, each of them supported by the testimony of more than one person. A summary of a few of these cases will illustrate the kind of material *Phantasms* contains.

A naval commander recalled an occurrence when he was 13 years old. He had nearly drowned when a boat attempting to land in rough sea on an island near Java was capsized. On coming to the surface after being repeatedly submerged, he called for his mother, which amused the men who rescued him. When he returned home some months later he told his family about his narrow escape including how, while he was in the water, he had had a distinct vision of his mother and sisters sitting at home and

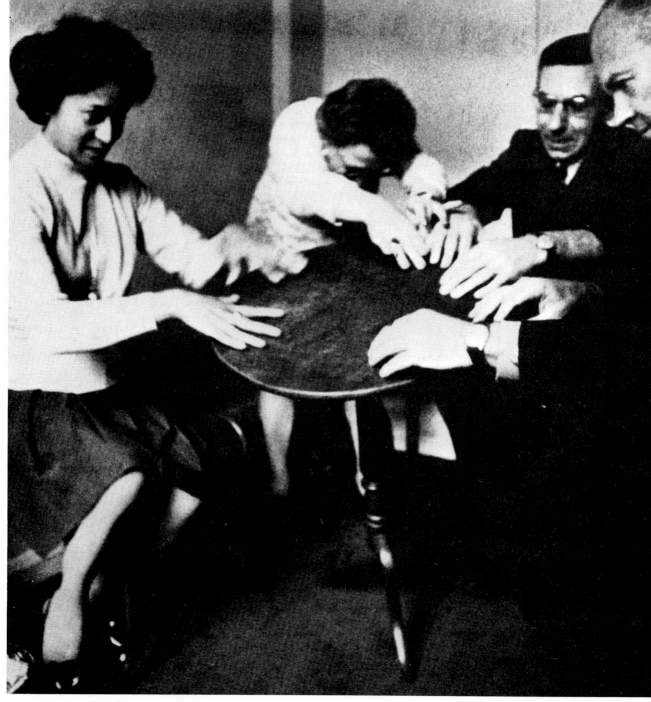

Above: an experiment by two skeptical science writers and two mediums to levitate a table. The table never did leave the floor, but it tilted and rocked itself so vigorously that people had to move out of its way.
Left: Colin Brookes-Smith sets up electronic apparatus to try to determine if the "lift" of a levitating table comes from below or above—the medium's knee perhaps if from below. His first results indicate it is from above.

Left: psychologist Edmund Gurney. He took part in the experiments conducted by the businessman Malcolm Guthrie, and was one of the most brilliant and respected of the early investigators. His death remains a puzzle in the history of psychical research, for in the middle of one project he committed suicide. Skeptics have suggested he had discovered all his work was in vain; others say the tragedy was the result of strictly personal complications.

of his mother sewing something white. They immediately recalled an occasion when they were all sitting just as he said and all had heard a repeated agonized cry of "Mother!" The experience had deeply troubled his mother, who had noted the date and time of it in a diary the next day. Allowing for the longitudinal difference in time between England and Java, the time they heard the cry was found to correspond exactly with the time of the boy's narrow escape.

Another case, involving an actual drowning, occurred in upstate New York in 1867. A little three-year-old girl was playing dolls one winter afternoon in a room where her father, mother, and aunt were also sitting. Suddenly she ran up to her aunt and exclaimed, "Auntie, Davie is drowned!" Davie was the child's cousin, a boy of nine, of whom she was very fond. He and his older brother lived about 25 miles away, and the little girl had not seen them for several months.

The adults had to ask the child to repeat herself twice before they understood what she was saying. Thinking the child didn't know the meaning of what she said, but wishing to avoid a morbid topic of conversation, the mother changed the subject. She did, however, make a note of the time: 4 p.m. A few hours later, the family received a telegram from the boys' father saying: "My little boys, Darius and Davie, were drowned at four o'clock today while skating at Kenks' Lake."

A local newspaper clipping obtained by the SPR researchers confirmed the date and approximate time of the accident.

A case that has been discussed and argued about ever since it was first published in *Phantasms of the Living* is the famous "Verity case." It is remarkable partly because it is well documented with supporting letters, and also because it contains elements of telepathy, clairvoyance, and possibly out-of-the-body projection.

Right: examples of the most successful results from the Guthrie series of experiments with thought transference during October and November 1883. There were about 150 trials altogether. The agents, all of them psychical researchers, would look at a drawing and afterward attempt to transfer the image mentally to the two blindfolded receivers, Miss Relph and Miss Edwards. They would remove the blindfold when they felt themselves ready, and would attempt to reproduce the drawing.

Response Drawing

S. H. Beard, a young man who was known and trusted by the officers of the SPR, gave Gurney an account of attempts he made to project himself in spirit into the presence of his fiancée, Miss L. S. Verity. "On a certain Sunday evening," he wrote, "having been reading of the great power which the human will is capable of exercising, I determined with the whole force of my being that I would be present in spirit in the front bedroom on the second floor of a house situated at 22 Hogarth Road, Kensington, in which slept two ladies of my acquaintance . . . The time at which I determined I would be there was one o'clock in the morning, and I also had a strong intention of making my presence perceptible."

A few days later, when he visited Miss Verity, she told him that at 1 a.m. on the night in question she had suddenly awakened and seen him distinctly, standing beside her bed. When he moved toward her she had screamed, awakening her young sister in the next bed, who also saw the apparition. After the figure had vanished Miss Verity called another sister from an adjoining room, and both girls described their vision of Beard, what he was wearing, and where he stood, in exactly the same terms. Gurney subsequently met all three girls, obtained signed statements from them, and carefully cross-examined them. He had no doubt that their testimony was truthful.

Beard tried the trick again about a year later when the Veritys were living in a house in Kew, another part of London. On this particular night his fiancée was sharing a bedroom with a married sister, who had only met Beard once at a ball two years before. It was this sister who saw the apparition of Beard when he projected himself into the bedroom. She wrote in her statement that she had not yet gone to sleep when she saw the door open and Beard enter the room. She said he came to her bedside and first took her hair in his hand, then took her hand in his and looked intently at the palm. Miss Verity was asleep at the time, and the married sister didn't wake her up and tell her about it until the apparition had gone. What the fiancée thought of this apparent fickleness on the part of the spirit of her intended is not on record.

Beard visited the sisters in Kew the following day. They were astonished when, after they had given him an account of the odd happening of the previous night, he produced from his pocket a paper on which he had written an account of his intentions and

his effort to project his image. He had not known that the sister would be visiting them when he conceived the idea.

Gurney again investigated and found the case well corroborated. Intrigued, he asked Beard to send him a note the next time he intended to attempt to project himself. Beard did so. However, he didn't see Miss Verity for two weeks after this attempt. When he did see her, she told him that she had distinctly seen him in her room at midnight on a certain date, and that he had stroked her hair. Beard couldn't remember whether the date she gave coincided with his attempt. But Gurney had Beard's letter stating his intention to appear that evening at a certain time, and by comparing this with Miss Verity's signed statement, he found that both the date and the time coincided. Coincidence of time is most important in such experiments, and in spontaneous apparitions as well. A time gap between the agent's effort to send the image and the seeing of the image by the percipient will tend to suggest that the apparition is a subjective hallucination by the percipient, weakening the case for its being telepathic.

In his discussion of the Verity case in *Phantasms of the Living*, Gurney noted a significant difference between such evidence for telepathy and the evidence obtained from controlled experiments. In the experimental situation the agent is thinking about the image or word or idea he is trying to project, and if the experiment is successful, the percipient receives an impression that is more or less a copy of the impression in the agent's mind. In the case of a willed apparition, such as the Beard experiments, the minds of agent and percipient are occupied in different ways. The agent is not so much thinking of his own image as mentally reaching out toward the percipient, trying to imagine where that person is at the moment, perhaps concentrating on their relationship. "It is thus probable," writes Gurney, "that the percipient's aspect has formed a larger part of the agent's whole idea than his own; yet it is *his* aspect, and nothing else, that is telepathically perceived." The same is true for crisis apparitions, even though the agent may not be consciously trying to project his image.

From this observation Gurney went on to draw a conclusion about the nature of the telepathic process. "As long as the impression in the percipient's mind is merely a reproduction of that in the agent's mind, it is possible to conceive some sort of physical basis for the fact of the transference." He cited several examples from physics, such as the way a permanent magnet brought into a room will magnetize any iron in that room, or the way an electric current in one wire will induce a current in a neighboring wire. As long as the information transmitted telepathically was essentially the same at either end—sending and receiving—it might be assumed to travel via some as yet undis-

Left: writer and teacher F. W. H. Myers. More than any other, Myers can probably be called the founder of psychical research. He made his resolve to study the possibility of communication with spirits of the dead after a starlight walk with Henry Sidgwick in 1869, and devoted the rest of his lifetime to dedicated research and careful reporting.

covered physical medium. But when the percipient saw something *different* from what the agent was thinking—for example, the image of the agent himself—a physical basis for telepathy seemed unlikely.

Another argument against a physical basis for telepathy was that all known physical forces were known to become weaker as they travel over great distances. This is not the case with telepathy. A telepathic message or apparition can be sent as easily across a continent as across a street. Recently, however, scientists have discovered that when certain metals are cooled to the temperature of liquid helium they will conduct an electric current with no loss due to resistance or the distance involved. The existence of these so-called "superconductors" has reintroduced the possibility that some physical force may be at work in cases of telepathy. Yet the nature of this force remains as much a mystery as when Gurney first discussed the problem nearly a hundred years ago.

Some of the peculiarities of telepathic transmission emerged in a series of more than 750 experiments performed between 1910 and 1924 by Professor Gilbert Murray of Oxford University. A small group of family and friends took part in the experiments. While Professor Murray was out of the room, one of them—usually the person chosen as agent—would choose some image or incident for him to guess. The subject announced would then be written down exactly by the participant taking notes. Murray would reenter the room, take the hand of the agent, and try to determine the subject chosen, while the note-taker recorded his efforts. The subjects were a colorful mixture of incidents from literature and history, sometimes including people known to the participants. Here is a typical example, with Murray's daughter, Mrs. Arnold Toynbee, as agent:

Mrs. Toynbee: "I'll think of Rupert [Brooke] meeting Natasha in *War and Peace*. Running in a yellow dress—running through a wood."

Professor Murray: "Well, I thought when I came into the room it was about Rupert. Yes, it's fantastic. He's meeting somebody out of a book. He's meeting Natasha in *War and Peace*. I don't know what he is saying—perhaps 'Will you run away with me?'."

Mrs. T.: "Can you get the scene?"

Professor M.: "No, I can't get it."

Great care was taken to insure that Professor Murray was out of earshot of the group. However, the possibility that hyperaesthesia (in this case a sharpening of the hearing faculty) could influence the results was considered by the experimenters. Murray himself noticed that while he was concentrating his attention on the experiment he became acutely sensitive to noises, and that perhaps he was subconsciously receiving aural stimuli from this group. On the few occasions when the subject was not spoken aloud within the group, Murray failed to identify it. Most of these failures, however, occurred during a run of failures in which the subject was usually spoken, so it may be that other factors contributed to the lack of success.

Those who reported on the experiments to the SPR noted that there were many successes that could not be attributed to hyper-

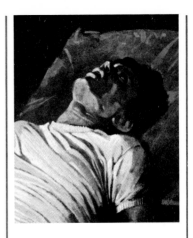

Mind Out of Body

Among the cases in the records of the Society for Psychical Research is the story of a distinguished Italian engineer. He wrote that one June, studying hard for his examinations, he had fallen into a deep deep sleep during which he apparently knocked over his kerosene lamp. Instead of going out, it gave off a dense smoke that filled the room. He gradually became aware that the thinking part of him had become entirely separate from his sleeping physical body. His independent mind recognized that to save his life he should pick up the fallen lamp and open the window. But he could not make his physical body wake up and respond in any way.

Then he thought of his mother, asleep in the next room, and he saw her clearly through the wall. He saw her hurriedly get up, go to the window, and throw it open as if carrying out the thought in his mind. He also saw her leave her room and come into his. She came to his body and touched it, and at her touch he was able to rejoin his physical body. He woke up with dry throat, throbbing temples, and a choking feeling.

Later his mother verified that she had opened the window before coming in to him—exactly as he had seen it through a solid wall.

acute hearing. Sometimes Murray would guess a scene from a book he had not read, and mention details about the scene or characters not spoken aloud when the subject was chosen. The only conceivable way he could have received this information was by telepathy with the agent, or with one of the other participants who knew the book.

A striking example of a miss that indicated a partial hit was an experiment in which a Mr. Mellor, acting as agent, said: "I'm thinking of the operating room in the nursing home in which I was operated [on]." Murray's response was: "I get an impression of a theater. No. I can't get it. I'm now guessing—Covent Garden and Oedipus." Although Mellor had used the phrase "operating *room*" rather than "operating theater," the concept of a theater

Left: Gilbert Murray, an Oxford University professor, was twice president of the SPR. He had a particular interest in telepathy, and did a series of telepathic experiments with members of his family.

of some kind had apparently been transmitted to Murray.

These experiments raise the possibility of telepathy being increased by the rapport existing between certain members of the same family—an aspect of parapsychology that is attracting some attention today. Murray seemed to be most successful when the agent was his daughter, Mrs. Toynbee. Whether this was due partly to a sympathetic relationship between them, or whether it was due to some exceptional ability of hers to concentrate on the subject remains an open question.

In evaluating the results of the experiments, the participants judged slightly over 33 percent to be complete successes; about 40 percent to be failures; and the remainder, partial successes. Of course, given the nature of the material used, judgments of success or failure were to some extent subjective. More accurate means of measuring telepathy were to be developed in the years that followed, as psychical research adopted more of the methods of the laboratory.

Below: an early experiment by Dr. J. B. Rhine at his Duke University laboratory tested the telepathic abilities of twins. While one concentrated on a picture in a separate room (right), the other tried to reproduce it (left). It was found that twins do better in transmitting telepathic messages to each other than unrelated persons. This goes a step farther than the Murray experiments, which seemed to show that family rapport could heighten telepathic powers. Rhine assumed that the extremely close rapport between twins would make them the most sensitive to telepathic communications.

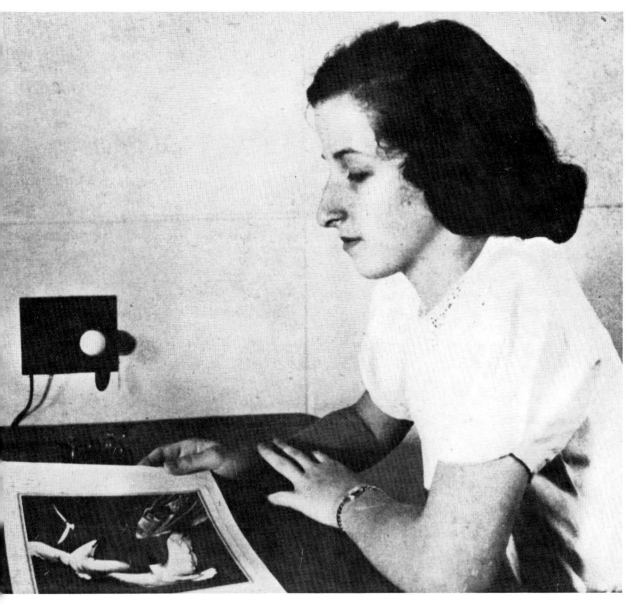

3

Harry Price and His Contemporaries

One winter evening in 1937 a group of six people were gathered together in a large house in a smart London suburb to witness an event which one of them later described as "the most remarkable case of materialization I have ever witnessed."

It took a lot to astonish Harry Price, who wrote these words, for he had been in psychical research for many years. He had sat with all the great mediums of Europe and America, and knew all the tricks of their trade. He had publicly denounced several of them when he had caught them cheating. But this "most remarkable" materialization was not produced by a professional medium.

By the turn of the 20th century, psychic phenomena had been investigated by many individuals of great eminence in various fields. Harry Price, who had some early training as an engineer, had a passion from the age of eight for magic and finding out how it worked. He became one of the most indefatigable investigators that psychical research has known. Right: a so-called spirit photograph of Harry Price in which a woman's figure showed up only on the developed picture. It was taken by William Hope, whom Price exposed as a fraud in 1922. Price stated flatly that not one of the many spirit photographs produced for him during his tests had ever been genuine.

47

"Price became aware of a presence between them..."

The group consisted of some women friends who gathered every Wednesday evening in this suburban house for a seance. Seances were, of course, being held all over London. What made this one remarkable, and of interest to Harry Price, was that the group claimed that one of their members' daughter, who had died 16 years before at the age of six, appeared physically in the room.

Price was skeptical but fascinated. He could see no reason why a private circle of respectable people should wish to perpetrate a fraud that would hold them up to ridicule if it were exposed. Nevertheless, he took all the precautions against fraud that he would have taken to an experimental sitting with a professional medium. Before the seance began he examined the room and its contents thoroughly, had all unnecessary furniture, ornaments, and pictures removed to another room, sprinkled starch powder on the floor on both sides of the door, and further insured that no one could enter the room by sealing the door and all the windows with masking tape. He initialled the tape so that if someone broke the seal and then reapplied other tape, he would be able to detect the substitution.

When the seance began the group sat in darkness for some 20 minutes and the bereaved mother, who was sitting next to Price, repeatedly whispered "Rosalie!" She sobbed quietly. Then she said, "My darling." Price became aware of a presence between them, and felt something soft and warm touch his hand, which was resting on his knee. Then he was given permission to touch the materialization. To his amazement he felt the nude figure of a little girl whose height he estimated at about three and a half feet. He felt her all over, put his ear to her chest and heard a heartbeat, and held her wrist in which he detected a fast-beating pulse. He was next allowed to examine the child by the light emitted from a luminous plaque which had been lying face down on the floor. His eyes confirmed what his hands had felt. Here was a pretty child, aged about six, with long hair falling over her shoulders. He asked her several questions, but the only one that got a reply was, "Rosalie, do you love your mummy?" Then the child lisped "Yes." The mother cried and clasped her to her breast, and all the women in the circle dissolved in tears. This highly charged emotional seance ended 15 minutes later, and when the lights were put on there was no sign of Rosalie. A thorough examination of the room, the seals, and the starch powder, showed that no one could have entered or left it during the seance.

This is a fairly extreme example of a type of story that continually turns up in the literature of psychical research, and that leaves the reader only with a choice of improbabilities. In this case the improbabilities are: a) that Price was lying and made the whole thing up; b) that he was successfully duped; c) that Rosalie was actually a genuine spirit materialization. That he was lying is improbable because he included the story in his book *Fifty Years of Psychical Research* only reluctantly, at his publisher's request; it is not a story that would help his reputation as a serious psychical researcher. A friend who saw Price on the day after the Rosalie seance described him as "visibly shaken" by the experience—an unlikely state of mind

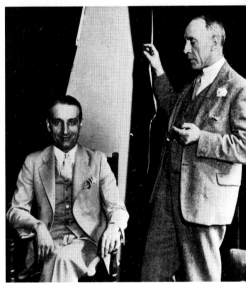

Left: one of Harry Price's precautions against fraud during a seance was to sprinkle starch powder to detect foot movements. He also marked chalk circles around such movable objects as the flower vase at top left.

Below: Price with Frank Decker, an American medium who agreed to undergo a series of tests in Price's laboratory in London. Under the stringent controls that Price contrived, Decker failed to produce any phenomena at all.

if he were lying. That Price was duped is improbable because he took elaborate precautions, knew all the methods employed by fraudulent materializing mediums, and was convinced that the mother's emotions were genuine. If the materialization was a hoax she too was a victim of it. The third supposition, that Rosalie was a materialization, is improbable because there is no precedent for such a phenomenon outside legend and folk-lore. It violates all known laws of nature.

The Rosalie case exemplifies the problem that scientists have when confronted with the evidence of psychical research. To be stuck with a choice between improbabilities is not a situation that holds out much hope for the advancement of knowledge. It is an understandable reaction to shrug off the problem and get on with other work.

But let us stay with the problem for a while. An odd thing about psychical research is that certain types of phenomena and certain avenues of research seem to prevail at particular

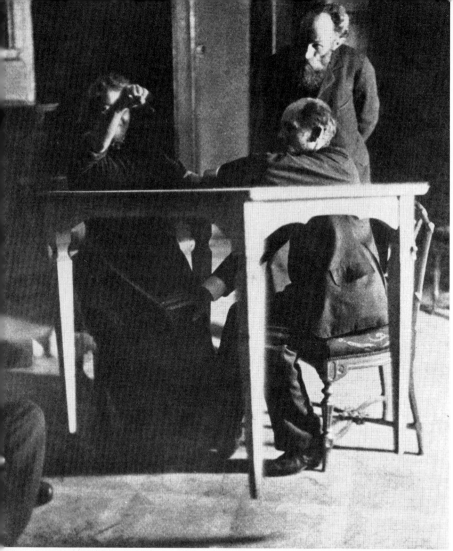

Fraud and physical mediumship
often seemed to be inseparable.
Above: Eusapia Palladino at one
of her seances. Even those who
supported her mediumship admitted
she would cheat on occasion.
Left: a medium's accomplice of
the 1890s, caught in the act
with his ectoplasm trousers down.

times. Levitations and materializations are not much heard of
nowadays, but both were frequently observed by the researchers
of the period between the two World Wars. The founding
members of the SPR, and its sister organization the American
SPR, preferred to investigate mental phenomena—telepathy
and clairvoyance—partly because experiments were easier to
control and their results easier to assess, and partly no doubt
because they were loath to demean themselves in the rough-and-
tumble of the seance room. Their colleagues in continental
Europe were less cautious, however, and apparently more
ready to put their professional reputations in jeopardy by
giving credence to the physical manifestations of mediumship.

On the subject of materializations, consider the words of

Professor Charles Richet, a distinguished French researcher and winner of the Nobel Prize for his contribution to physiology: "I shall not waste time in stating the absurdities, almost the impossibilities, from a psycho-physiological point of view, of this phenomenon. A living being, or living matter, formed under our eyes, which has its proper warmth, apparently a circulation of blood, and a physiological respiration, which has also a kind of psychic personality having a will distinct from the will of the medium, in a word, a new human being! This is surely the climax of marvels! Nevertheless, it is a fact."

No doubt Professor Richet was willing to commit himself so unequivocally because he was supported by distinguished contemporaries. His compatriots Dr. Gustave Geley and Dr.

Above: spirit phenomena were similar no matter where they occurred. Shown is a Danish seance during which a levitating chair sailed past the heads of sitters.

51

Above: Charles Richet, the noted physiologist and psychical researcher who went to Algiers to investigate Eva C. and her materialization of Bien Boa, a long dead Brahmin Hindu. Richet remained committed to his belief in her mediumship even after subsequent investigators were unimpressed by her capabilities.

Eugene Osty, the German physician Baron von Schrenck-Notzing, the great English physicists Sir William Crookes and Sir Oliver Lodge, were all convinced that they had witnessed genuine materializations under strictly controlled conditions. They could have been wrong. Nobel Prize winners and eminent physicists are no better qualified than anyone else to see through the wiles and sleight of hand of a clever conjuror. But that they were wrong *all* the time, and that *all* the phenomena they saw produced by mediums were fraudulent, is difficult to believe when one reads some of the accounts of their experiences and of the precautions they took against fraud. It is also difficult to imagine how some of the mediums, particularly the young women, could possibly have gotten access to the jealously guarded secrets of professional conjurors.

One of the most controversial physical mediums of the early 20th century was Eva Carriere (known in psychical research as Eva C.). Her real name was Marthe Beraud. The daughter of a high-ranking French army officer, she was brought up in Algiers. Her psychic powers were discovered by a general, who invited Professor Richet to investigate. Richet was impressed by what he saw—the full-form materialization of an individual who called himself Bien Boa. Although Richet noted a certain artificial quality about Bien Boa's beard, he remained convinced that the figure was produced paranormally by the medium. Subsequently, an Arab servant confessed that he was the spirit Bien Boa, and this confession was corroborated by Mlle. Beraud. However, her confession described a kind of trickery seemingly impossible to achieve under the conditions imposed by Richet, and Richet claimed that her statement simply indicated the mental instability typical of mediums.

A few years later Marthe Beraud appeared in Paris, where she produced impressive psychic phenomena. They were studied by a number of eminent researchers including Schrenck-Notzing—who gave her the pseudonym Eva C.—and Gustave Geley. She was also studied by the British SPR with less remarkable results. The most positive results were obtained by the French investigators, and in his book *Clairvoyance and Materialization* Geley published a series of photographs of materializations allegedly produced by Eva while in a trance. Some of the pictures show amorphous doughy masses, and others are of fully formed human heads. In a solemn and level-headed accompanying text Geley relates how on many occasions he saw a material substance (which Richet called "ectoplasm") emanate from various parts of Eva's body and form itself into organic shapes which were solid to the touch. Again we are faced with the problem of choosing to believe whether the distinguished professors were liars or the victims of a hoax, or whether, as they claimed, an actual materialization took place. Of course, no scientist is going to accept as evidence a man's sworn testimony on a phenomenon that violates the known laws of nature, even if that man is a Nobel Prize winner. He wants to see a repeatable experiment before he will acknowledge a fact proved, and one trouble with materialization is that the evidence for it cannot be produced on demand. Those who believe in it claim that it is a spontaneous phenomenon, and that

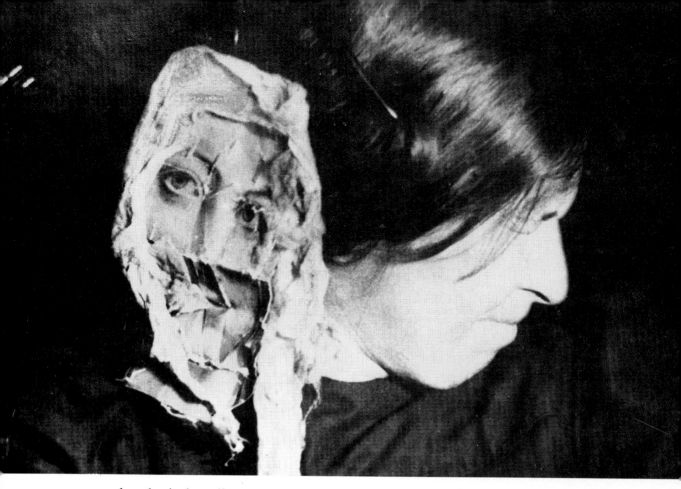

one reason why physical mediums have sometimes cheated is that pressure has been put on them to produce the phenomena to order. Only when the effects do not come spontaneously, they say, does the medium resort to trickery.

Eva C.'s effects were almost commonplace compared to those produced by Franek Klusky. According to Geley, who devoted a large section of his book to him, Klusky was the supreme physical medium of the age. He was a Polish poet and banker who only discovered his strange gifts at the age of 46, and was at first reluctant to exploit them. Finally, he was persuaded to participate in serious research. He certainly produced some bizarre effects. During a seance a bowl of paraffin wax, kept at melting point by being floated on warm water, was put near him. When a human form materialized it was asked to plunge a hand, a foot, or part of a face into the wax several times, then to plunge again in a bowl of cold water to set the wax. When the form dematerialized a wax molding of it would remain. This could be filled with plaster, and in this way several casts of spirit hands and feet were obtained, photographs of which are in Geley's book. In his accounts of the seances, Geley says there was no possibility that Klusky could have produced these effects fraudulently, for he was closely observed, and both his hands were held all the time. Moreover, the wrist openings of the wax "gloves" were too narrow for a living hand to have slipped through without breaking the mold. When the "spirit" hands were examined by experts they were found to be smaller than the hands of anyone who had been present at the seance.

Above: Eva C. producing the materialization of an ectoplasmic face. The course of Eva C.'s mediumship was spectacular and highly controversial. By the time of her seances—from the 1900s to the 1920s—test controls had become so rigid that she was often made to sit in the nude. She even had emetics administered to check that she had not swallowed any material for faking her effects.

Below: Baron A. von Schrenk-Notzing also worked with Eva C.

Left: Gustave Geley, who obtained the famous plaster casts of the hands said to be materialized by Polish medium Franek Klusky.

Right: one of several wax molds of materialized hands produced by Klusky. Spirits around the seance table were challenged to plunge their hands into a bowl of wax kept at melting point on the seance table. Plaster would then be poured into the mold.

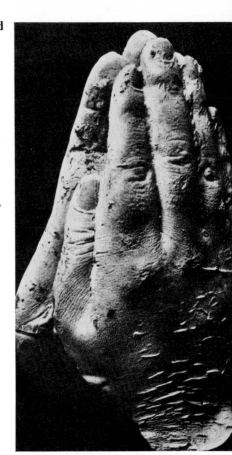

Below: Klusky during a seance with a buzzard he materialized perched calmly on his shoulders.

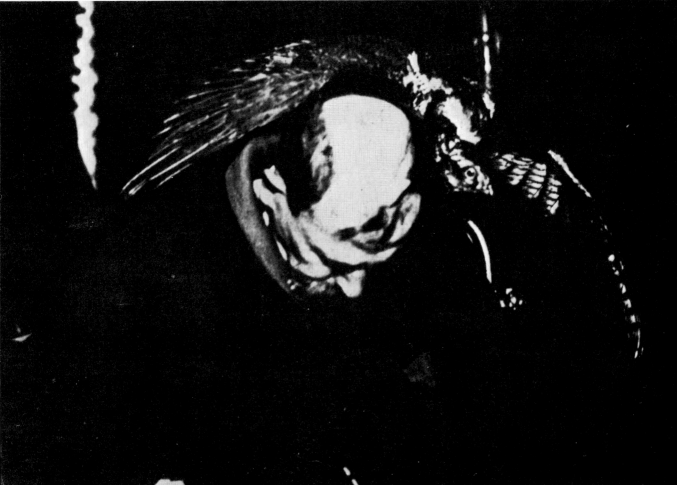

Klusky also produced materializations of animals. It was not uncommon for cats, dogs, squirrels, and birds to appear in the room. Geley's book contains a picture of Klusky with an immense materialized buzzard on his shoulders. But the most alarming experience for the sitters must have been the appearance of a creature they called *Pithecanthropus*, a large hairy ape man who grunted, ground his teeth, lurched around the room, and tried to lick the hands and faces of everybody present.

Klusky produced similar effects independently both for the French investigators and for the Polish SPR, but he would not sit with Harry Price. Price declared that Klusky's mediumship "is unsatisfactory from the point of view that no scientific body has investigated the alleged miracles." This must have annoyed Geley and Richet, who considered that their investigations were scientifically unimpeachable. For example, in order to insure that the "spirit gloves" obtained at Klusky's seances were actually made during the experiment and with their wax, the researchers mixed a small amount of a certain chemical with the wax. This chemical—undetectable at the time of the experiment—would later produce a discoloration in the wax when it was treated in a certain way. Richet was convinced that this and all the other evidence for the reality of materialization added up to a scientifically proved case. He wrote: "The fact that intelligent forces are projected from an organism that can act mechanically, can move objects and make sounds, is a phenomenon as certainly established as any fact in physics." He did not consider that this constituted a proof of survival of the spirit after death, however. He inclined rather to the view that materializations were thought-forms projected by the medium or in some cases, perhaps unconsciously, by one of the sitters participating in the seance.

That some kind of energy discharge takes place, both from the medium and from the sitters, during a physical seance was a hypothesis widely discussed during this period. In some sittings he conducted with a young London nurse named Stella Cranshaw, Price obtained objective evidence indicating that energy was absorbed from the environment during a seance. Self-recording thermometers showed a considerable drop in temperature—on one occasion as much as 11°F—and this drop coincided with the occurrence of the more vigorous physical manifestations, such as levitations. At the end of the seance the room temperature was always marginally higher than at the start, which was to be expected on account of the presence of the sitters. But the dramatic drop coinciding with the climax of the seance would seem to suggest that energy was somehow borrowed from the environment to produce the effects and then paid back at the end. Here, it seemed, was a genuine hard paranormal fact, a phenomenon objectively recorded, impossible to fake, showing the operation of a physical law quite unknown to contemporary science. It has not been satisfactorily explained to this day.

Harry Price was a prolific inventor of ingenious devices for making his research methods foolproof and scientifically acceptable. To test Stella's powers to move objects by psychic force

The Apelike Spirit

In 1920 the Polish medium Franek Klusky had a series of sittings with the International Metaphysical Institute, among whose prominent members were the French investigators Professor Charles Richet and Gustave Geley. The seance circle sat with hands linked, and the expert researchers kept the medium under careful observation. Unlike many mediums, Klusky did not go into trance during a seance. He worked in a state of full consciousness, but with deep concentration.

Klusky was noted for a remarkable ability to materialize both humans and animals. His most electrifying seances were those in which strange forms loomed out of the darkness— on one occasion a great hulking creature halfway between human and ape. It was about the stature of a man, but had a simian face, long arms, and hair all over. It smelled, sitters said, like a wet dog. Once the big hairy head leaned heavily on a sitter's shoulder. Another sitter put out a hand, which the creature licked with a large soft tongue.

The scientifically minded sitters called Klusky's materialized apeman *Pithecanthropus*. Geley believed totally in the medium's psychic powers. On the other hand, British psychic researcher Harry Price doubted his abilities.

he constructed his "telekinetoscope." This elaborate invention contained two electrical contacts that normally required a two-ounce pressure to bring them together. They were protected from physical interference by a soap bubble, a glass shade, and a cage. When the electrical contact was made a red bulb would light up. At her first attempt Stella succeeded in completing the circuit and lighting the bulb, and when the telekinetoscope was examined, both the glass shade and the soap bubble were found intact. She had apparently brought the two electrical contacts together by the exertion of psychic force.

Most of Price's complicated inventions were designed to control the medium and prevent fraud. He had an "electric chair" in which the medium sat with head, arms, feet, hands, and seat all in contact with electric light circuits. At any movement a red signal light was automatically switched off. To insure further that psychokinetic effects were genuinely produced by psychic forces he developed his "counterpoise table." The object to be moved psychokinetically, which could be as light as a handkerchief, was placed on one side of the table. When the object was lifted, the other side of the table would fall, closing an electrical circuit that immediately activated a battery of cameras. Whatever moved the object would, if it were visible, be automatically photographed. Later Price devised a system of infrared ray projectors in the ceiling and walls of the seance room, which provided a more sophisticated and satisfactory method of control than the inhibiting electric chair. Each projector was aligned with a photoelectric cell. When mediums took position in a chair, certain rays were obscured by their body, and the resulting pattern was recorded in a nearby control room. Even if a medium were left entirely alone in the seance room, every movement could be observed on the control panel, which would also register the movement of any object in

Above: Stella C., the medium discovered on a train by Harry Price. She was apparently not greatly interested in her psychic powers, and only reluctantly took part in Price's various experiments. In spite of rigorous controls she produced electrifying effects. Right: a chart of temperatures showing Stella C.'s remarkable quality of causing the room temperature to fall during a seance—apparently by absorbing the energy to produce the effects.

No.	Date of Sitting	Time of Start	Temp. at Start	Time of Finish	Temp. at Finish	Min. (intermediate)	Fall	Rise
1	Mar. 22	11.32 a.m.	60°	12.35 p.m.	62°	49°	11°	13°
2	Mar. 29	11.38 a.m.	61°	12.47 p.m.	65°	49.5°	11.5°	15.5°
3	April 5	11.20 a.m.	64.5°	12.43 p.m.	65°	57°	7.5°	8°
4	April 12	11.20 a.m.	62°	1.3 p.m.	66°	58°	4°	8°
5	April 19	11.18 a.m.	63.5°	1.15 p.m.	64.5°	43°	20.5°	21.5°
6	May 3	11.40 a.m.	67°	1.45 p.m.	74°	no fall		7°
7	May 10	11.5 a.m.	58.5°	12.25 p.m.	64°	57°	1.5°	7°
8	May 17	11.0 a.m.	57.5°	12.55 p.m.	64°	57°	0.5°	7°
9	May 24	11.15 a.m.	59°	12.55 p.m.	65°	58°	1°	7°
10	June 7	11.6 a.m.	62.5°	12.55 p.m.	68.5°	61.75°	0.75°	6.75°
11	June 21	11.15 a.m.	63.5°	12.45 p.m.	68.5°	62.5°	1°	6°
12	Sept. 27	10.45 a.m.	61°	12.35 p.m.	64°	no fall		3°
13	Oct. 4	10.40 a.m.	56°	12.35 p.m.	59°	55.5°	.5°	3.5°

TABLE OF TEMPERATURES

the room. In this way, not only was the medium controlled, but also any physical phenomena produced were automatically visible to the observer.

Obviously, such sophisticated apparatus required some form of permanent housing, and in 1926 Price opened his National Laboratory of Psychical Research in Kensington. One of the first subjects to be studied there was the Rumanian peasant girl Eleonore Zügun.

Eleonore was 12 years old when the weird effects that made her famous started to happen. In her presence, objects would fly about with no visible agent having thrown them. In other words, she was the focus of poltergeist activity. It seems unlikely that she would have tried to create the phenomena fraudulently, for because of them she was at first persecuted by the superstitious villagers who thought they were the work of the Devil. Eleonore was put in an asylum, where she might have remained had she not come to the attention of an Austrian Countess who was interested in psychic matters. The Countess secured her release, took her to Vienna, and wrote an article about her that was published in the Journal of the American Society for Psychical Research. When Harry Price read the article he decided to go to Vienna to investigate the phenomena for himself.

His investigation started with a rather alarming incident. He, Eleonore, and the Countess were in the latter's study-bedroom in her apartment. He had brought the child a toy which came apart while she was playing with it. She ran over to where he and the Countess were sitting and asked them to fix the toy. They rose to attend to it, and while they were doing so a long steel paper knife shot across the room from behind them, just missing Price's head, and hit the door opposite. It clearly couldn't have been thrown by anyone, for there was no one else

Below: for its time, the Price laboratory in South Kensington, London, possessed remarkably sophisticated equipment designed to monitor seances and to detect any fraud. This photograph was taken in 1926, showing Price at work on one of his investigations.

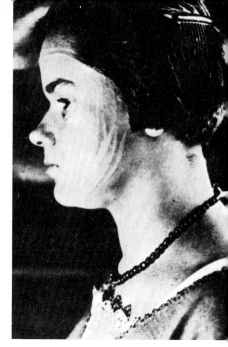

Above: Eleonore Zügun, the Rumanian child medium of 13, often had mysterious marks appear on her face—which she explained as the work of the Devil. She was one of Harry Price's first subjects for psychical research.

Above left: Eleonore with the Countess Zoe Wassilko-Serecki, who adopted her when she was being persecuted by her native villagers for her strange gifts.

Below: teethmarks such as these on Eleonore's hand were also said to be the work of the Devil.

in the room, and the writing desk where it had lain was across the room in front of a window that was securely fastened.

Several other movements of objects in the room occurred during Price's brief visit, and he was so impressed that he persuaded the Countess to bring Eleonore to London. There, in the National Laboratory, under carefully controlled conditions and in front of some distinguished witnesses, numerous PK effects were recorded. One odd feature of these events was that they were accompanied by stigmata on the child's body. Red weals and what looked like teeth marks would appear. Her pulse rate rose in proportion to the violence of the phenomena. Eleonore must have been greatly relieved when, at the onset of puberty, the phenomena abruptly stopped.

Eleonore's case is a classic example of poltergeist activity, in that the events were spontaneous, uncontrolled, and unpredictable. A girl who suffered similarly when she was 12 but who retained her psychic powers in adult life was the Danish medium Anna Rasmussen. She was studied intensively between 1922 and 1928 by Professor Winther of Copenhagen, who in 1927 invited Price to witness a demonstration at his laboratory.

Anna had a "trance personality" (or "spirit guide" as Spiritualists would say) named "Dr. Lasaruz," who supposedly brought about the movement of objects. In order to study these psychic powers, Professor Winther used a special device of a sealed glass case in which a number of pendulums of different weights were suspended by silk threads. In a sunlit room, under strict controls and before witnesses, Anna could make any one of the pendulums move in any direction as requested. All the experimenter had to do was ask Dr. Lasaruz to move a specific pendulum in a particular direction, and it would move accordingly. In his autobiography, Price wrote that he had never seen a more convincing example of psychokinesis than this.

The most famous psychics of the 1920s and 1930s were the Schneider brothers, Willi and Rudi. Like Hitler, they were born in the Austrian village of Braunau. From an early age the brothers showed remarkable psychic powers, and news of the so-called miracles taking place in Braunau reached Baron von Schrenck-Notzing. One of these miracles, witnessed and reported by retired warship commander Fritz Kogelnik, was the full materialization of Willi's spirit control "Olga," who "danced the tango very correctly and gracefully." Willi was the elder brother and the first to show psychic powers. In order to study Willi's powers thoroughly, Schrenck-Notzing arranged for the boy to go to Munich, train for the dental profession at his own expense, and be available for psychical research experiments. He invited colleagues and scientists from all over Europe to attend the experiments, and in 1922 Harry Price did so.

The control conditions imposed in Schrenck-Notzing's seance room involved the use of a large wooden cage with gauze panels. A heavy table, a hand bell, and a heavy music box—all marked with luminous paint so that their movements could be seen in the semidarkness—were placed inside the cage, which was then locked. Willi was controlled by being dressed in one-piece black tights outlined with luminous bands and buttons. Luminous bracelets were put on his wrists, and he was held firmly by two men.

Soon after Willi had gone into trance the table inside the locked cage gave a resounding bump on the floor, and was seen to rise. Then the music box began to play and bump up and down. The music would stop and resume at the command of any of the sitters, and when the music box had run down it was rewound by some unseen agency—an operation that normally required two hands, one to hold the box and the other to work the lever. Then the luminous hand bell rang and jumped about inside the cage. Other phenomena occurred outside the cage. Price dropped a handkerchief on the floor, and it rose in the air. A hand-like form appeared, waved to the sitters, then slowly dematerialized.

Later Schrenck-Notzing discovered that Rudi Schneider's powers were even greater than Willi's, and he arranged similar tests of the younger boy. Price went to Munich again to see Rudi, and eventually brought the boy to London to be investigated in Price's own Laboratory.

That the Schneider brothers' effects were genuine was formally attested by more than 100 distinguished scientists and other scholars who attended Schrenck-Notzing's demonstrations. Nevertheless, they were not above cheating. On one occasion the cameras linked to Price's counterpoise table caught Rudi in the act of manually removing a handkerchief which, without

Above: another child medium was Anna Rasmussen, whose powers developed when she was 12. Unlike Eleonore's, however, hers lasted past puberty into her adulthood.

Below: the pendulums suspended from hooks in this sealed glass case were successfully made to move by young Anna Rasmussen.

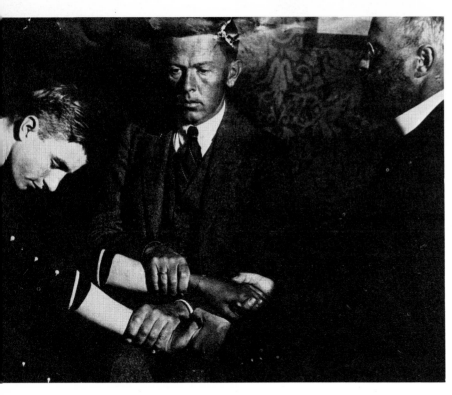

Left: Schrenck-Notzing tried to assure easy detection of fraud by dressing medium Willi Schneider in a tight one-piece costume and adorning him with luminous pins and bracelets. Two researchers also held Willi's hands firmly.

Right: Willi Schneider's brother Rudi. He took over Willi's spirit control, Olga, at the age of 11, and from that time Willi's powers declined and Rudi's developed. According to Price, he became "the most convincing physical medium of whom we have any record." After about 1932, his powers also seemed to fade.

Far right: Price's fraud-detector table used in a Schneider seance. The handkerchief is moving up apparently without human help.

the resulting photograph, would have been thought to have moved by paranormal means. (There is, however, some doubt about the authenticity of this photo.) In spite of this apparent evidence of cheating, Price was convinced that in most of his seances with Rudi—particularly those at which the electrical-contact method of control was used, as it always was after this incident—the PK affects were genuine. During many of Rudi's seances the automatic thermograph recorded a significant fall in temperature in the room, as it did at the Stella Cranshaw sittings.

In his autobiography Harry Price stated several times that he "would go a long way to see a miracle." Some of his critics have said that he sometimes went too far, pursuing his investigations in areas that only brought psychical research into disrepute. Any estimate of his contribution to knowledge of the paranormal must allow for the fact that there was a streak of the publicity seeker in him. He loved to be in the limelight, and he had a nose for a good story that would appeal to the press. But personal profit was not among his motives, for he funded most of his research work himself and he donated the National Laboratory, which cost him a substantial sum to set up, along with his personal library of 17,000 volumes, to the University of London. He had the courage not to mind making a fool of himself, and he justified his more outlandish investigations with the argument that any alleged miracle was worth looking into if only to prove there was nothing in it. In this way, one could separate the hard core of the genuinely paranormal from the mass of superstition, fraud, and delusion that surrounded and obscured it.

In 1931 an old German magical manuscript entitled *The Blocksberg Tryst* fell into Price's hands. He was immediately

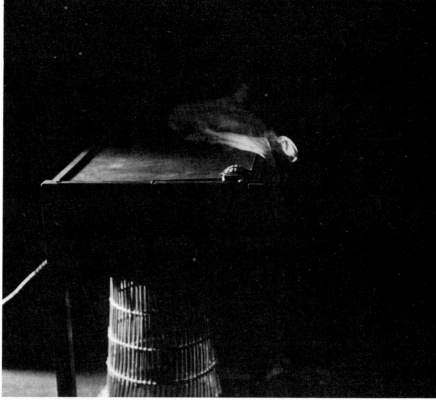

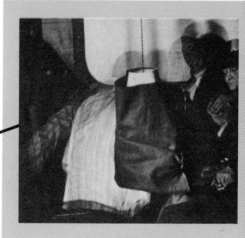

Above and left: the famous Price double-exposure showing Rudi in an act of fraud. His arm in the pajama jacket he wore at seances is apparently reaching out to take a handkerchief from the table and drop it on the floor— which would have been assumed to be the result of paranormal forces without the photograph. A detail of Rudi is above. There was considerable controversy about this picture. It was said that Price had faked it out of jealousy because his protege was working with other investigators.

Right: this magical manuscript entitled *The Blocksberg Tryst* inspired Harry Price and Dr. C. E. M. Joad to set off for an adventure on the Brocken, highest peak of Germany's Harz Mountains. The ritual described in this excerpt from an old German book of black magic called for a goat and a maiden pure in heart. Price explained that the experiment had been carried out "in connection with the Goethe Centenary celebrations" of 1932.

Below: Price in close study of *The Blocksberg Tryst* manuscript.

interested, and, to the dismay of his scientific friends, he announced his intention of going to the Brocken, the highest peak in the Harz Mountains in central Germany, to carry out an experiment in ritual magic. One friend who was not dismayed and fell in with the plan with enthusiasm was the philosopher Dr. C. E. M. Joad, and in January 1932 the two improbable "magicians" set off for Germany. The ritual required the participation of a "maiden pure in heart" and a white goat, and it involved various incantations, magic formulae, and the preparation of a magic circle and a special ointment composed of bats' blood, scrapings of church bells, soot, and honey. Catching bats proved a hazardous and difficult exercise, but finally all the preparations were completed, and they had only to wait for a night when there was a full moon visible from the top of

Left: Fräulein Urta Bohn, the "maiden pure in heart" found by Price and Dr. Joad for the magic rite on the Brocken. Right: preliminary experiments with Urta Bohn, Price, Joad, and the goat while waiting for the appropriate night to come. Below: the participants and their audience during the ritual. In spite of the best efforts of the two self-styled magicians, the goat didn't turn into a handsome young man as it was supposed to.

the Brocken. But month after month the moon was obscured by mist at the crucial time, and it was only after several postponements that the ritual was finally staged. If it worked, the "maiden pure in heart" would be rewarded by having the white goat transformed into a "youth of surpassing beauty." Needless to say, the goat remained a goat, and the newspapers had a field day. Price and Joad, however, returned to England satisfied that they had struck a blow for sanity and science by discrediting ritual magic and its devotees. The playwright Bernard Shaw expressed a general opinion of the experiment when he said that he might have been amused to be there but he "would not dream of making a special journey to see anything so silly!"

That Price was unashamed and unrepentant was proved by the fact that he undertook another and perhaps even sillier

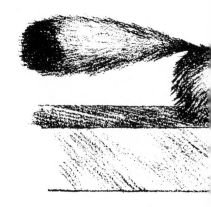

Above: the hole said to be used by Gef the talking mongoose—which could recite and sing—to enter the Irving home on the Isle of Man.

Left: Mr. Irving and his daughter on the doorstep of their farmhouse. The Gef affair was one of the most bizarre of Price's investigations.

Below: Gef the talking mongoose, drawn from a description given by the farmer who discovered it. The animal kept entirely out of sight during Price's investigatory visit.

journey a short time after the Brocken adventure. A correspondent in the Isle of Man informed him that a strange talking animal had attached itself to a family living in a farmhouse on the top of a mountain in the center of the island. Price wrote to the farmer, who confirmed that the animal was an Indian mongoose, and that it could not only talk but also converse intelligently, recite nursery rhymes and sing hymns. A friend of Price's, a Captain Macdonald, offered to investigate. When he returned from the island he reported that he had heard the "talking mongoose"—indeed had been verbally insulted by it—but had been unable even to catch a glimpse of it, and was unimpressed by the "phenomena." Reports of the mongoose's marvelous doings continued to reach Price, however, and some time later he investigated the matter for himself. He was hospitably received by the farmer and regaled with tales of "Gef's" marvels and mischief, but the "talking mongoose of Manx" remained as elusive as ever, and Price returned to London without any evidence of its existence. Nevertheless, he managed to write a book, *The Haunting of Cashen's Gap*, about the case.

When Price died in 1948, an era in psychical research came to an end. His flamboyance and his flair for publicity had embarrassed some of his colleagues, but he had been a key figure in the field for a quarter of a century. His energy, enthusiasm, curiosity, and independence were qualities that enabled him to function as a link-man between American, British, and European researchers. And in the course of his own investigations he had turned up enough well-attested inexplicable phenomena to give the most thoroughgoing skeptic food for thought.

4

ESP in the Laboratory

The scene is a room in the University of London. The year is 1937. A few people are about to engage in an elaborate guessing game, directed by the distinguished mathematician Dr. S. G. Soal. The person who is to do the guessing is Frederick Marion, a well-known stage telepathist.

Dr. Soal begins the game by handing Marion a small white handkerchief. Marion holds the handkerchief for a few seconds, hands it to one of the experimenters, and leaves the room accompanied by Soal and one of the other participants. The door, which has no keyhole, is closed behind them. The next stage of the game is to hide the

Scientific investigation of psi manifestations has come a long way from the darkened seance room with one researcher gripping a medium's hands and another holding his or her feet. Today experiments are conducted in the impersonal, controllable confines of a laboratory, and subjects are set specific tasks like matching a sequence of numbers or picking out the order of a pack of cards. Right: an experiment by the American Society for Psychical Research. The person behind the curtain is trying to guess one chosen square out of 25 squares. The experimenter, in another room, watches him on closed-circuit TV and tries to influence the choice by her concentration.

"Marion goes to the correct box ...and removes the handkerchief"

handkerchief in one of six tin boxes which are located in various places in the room and numbered one through six. One of the group rolls a die in a box, silently showing the upturned face of the die to the recorder, who makes a note of its number. The handkerchief is then placed in the box whose number corresponds to the number on the die.

One of the participants now pulls over his head a stockinette hood that covers his features, and steps into a curious contraption—a kind of sentry box on wheels, open at the front. Another person slots into the front of the box several pieces of plywood, until the only visible part of the man in the box is his covered head. All of the participants except the man in the sentry box now step behind a curtain. The curtain contains eyeholes, which enable them to see what follows.

Dr. Soal, Marion, and the other experimenter reenter the room. While Soal observes the proceedings carefully, Marion begins to walk around the room, trying to guess which of the boxes contains the handkerchief. He is followed by the man in the sentry box, who is wheeled by the other participant. Of the three people Marion can see, the only one who knows where the handkerchief is hidden is the man in the sentry box. As Marion walks around the room he frequently glances at the hooded head of this man. Eventually he goes to the correct box, lifts its lid, and removes the handkerchief.

This bizarre looking procedure was the final variation in a series of experimental games devised by Soal to determine whether Marion's ability to find hidden objects was in fact due to telepathy. The experiments had started out rather simply, with the half dozen or so participants remaining in the room seated around a table and watching Marion as he walked around the room trying to guess the correct box. Under these conditions he had guessed right 38 times out of 91 trials. The odds against scoring this high by chance are nearly 71 million to one.

It seemed probable, however, that Marion's success might be due not to telepathy but to physical cues from the sitters—cues they gave him unconsciously. In an effort to determine if this was the case and to what extent Marion depended upon such cues, Soal introduced various controls to obstruct cues from being given in the game: a curtain to hide all but one of the sitters; various kinds of hoods to cover the face of the person following Marion; cardboard boxes to cover his body down to his ankles. Even under these conditions, Marion continued to score high. It seemed possible that he was getting clues from another person's footsteps—the hesitations, accelerations, starts, stops. Hence the sentry box on wheels, eliminating telltale footsteps. Using the wooden panels, Soal varied the amount of coverage of the man's body. In the next-to-last series of experiments the front of the box was completely covered except for a tiny chink between the panels, through which the man could watch Marion and presumably will him to select the right tin box. Under these conditions, Marion's score dropped to chance level. With no cues, his apparent telepathic powers disappeared. In the final series, in which the man's hooded head was visible, they returned.

Dr. Soal's experiments with Marion clearly demonstrated

Above: Frederick Marion, the gifted stage telepathist who took part in tests with Dr. S. G. Soal.

Above: one of the Soal tests
with Marion, shown at the Harry
Price Laboratory. He is trying
to guess which is the preselected
playing card. Dr. S. G. Soal is
seated next to Marion in the
center of the experimental group.

Above: Soal during one of his
nightclub performances, as drawn
by the artist Feliks Topolski
in the early months of 1940.
Left: Soal's sentry box. In it
stood the one man in the room
who knew where some given item
was hidden. By removing or
replacing the wooden panels,
Soal could control how much of
the man could be seen—and so
determine to what extent he was
giving Marion unconscious signals.

Above: ESP tricks on stage are not new—in 1847 Robert Houdin (from whom Houdini took his stage name) was packing them in with feats of mind reading on stage before admiring audiences.

that the man's extraordinary ability was not telepathy but an acute sensitivity to involuntary cues given by his audience—in this case by the hooded man in the sentry box.

"Let's not talk about extrasensory perception," say the critics of the ESP hypothesis, "until we know all that there is to know about sensory perception." Perhaps we will find that all the so-called paranormal powers of the human mind are just normal powers heightened to an extreme degree. Because telepathy, clairvoyance, and precognition appear to contradict our basic ideas of physics, time, and space, we certainly ought not to jump to the conclusion that they occur until we have exhausted every other possible explanation of the phenomena, goes the argument.

Laboratory research into ESP in the universities began in the 1930s, and it took full account of the skeptics' arguments. It was conducted by men trained in scientific method, and they understood clearly that no amount of spontaneous evidence would convince science of the reality of phenomena that conflicted with its basic assumptions. A telepathic apparition of one's cousin at the exact moment his plane is shot down, or a precognitive dream of the San Francisco earthquake, might be dramatic evidence of psi at work, but it is not the kind of evidence needed to convince a scientist. What was needed was to bring ESP into the laboratory where it could be observed and measured, and where experiments could be designed, as in the physical sciences, to test hypotheses about it.

The pioneer in this work was Dr. J. B. Rhine. In 1927 he and his wife Louisa, who had both taken Ph.D. degrees in botany, went to Duke University in North Carolina to pursue post-doctoral study in psychical research, They chose Duke because its Professor of Psychology, William McDougall—formerly President of both the British and the American SPR—had publicly campaigned for psychical research to become a university study, and was able to offer them his personal advice and the facilities of his department.

Six years later Rhine published his book *Extra-Sensory*

Right: the calling card of Lady the talking horse. She picked successes in races, presidential campaigns, and on the stock market. She also located missing persons, spelling out the name of the place where they would be found. Dr. J. B. Rhine camped in a field to study her, and declared she had psychic abilities. But other investigators suggested it was all a case of the horse following almost imperceptible commands of her owner, Mrs. Fonda. Whether Mrs. Fonda was psychic or not was never tested.

PHONE

82-0478

ADMISSION
ADULT $1, CHILD 50c
INCLUDING TAX

LADY WONDER
THE EDUCATED MIND READING HORSE
WILL ANSWER QUESTIONS
MRS. C. D. FONDA
PETERSBURG PIKE AND RUFFIN ROAD
OPEN EVERY AFTERNOON AND ~~EVENING~~
4TH HOUSE ON RIGHT

Perception, which gave an account of the first years of parapsychological research at Duke. In scientific circles it was almost
as great a bombshell of a book as Darwin's *Origin of Species*
had been, and it stirred up a scientific controversy that is still
raging.

The anecdotal evidence for ESP, such as that published in
Gurney's *Phantasms of the Living*, suggests that it is a spontaneous
faculty, often connected with crisis situations such as disasters
and deaths. If this were true, then getting ESP to work under
laboratory conditions would be virtually impossible. However,
it is a basic principle of scientific research that small events
produced in the laboratory can establish theoretical principles
relevant to much larger events. Men never understood thunder-
storms until they discovered in the laboratory that sparks are
produced between electrically charged objects. Similarly, an
apparently trivial example of ESP, such as guessing what is on a
card more often than chance would account for, might lead us to
the principle underlying more dramatic spontaneous cases of
ESP. It was in the hope of finding such a principle that Rhine
began his research program at Duke University. It did not
matter if the ESP effects produced in the laboratory were small
and relatively undramatic. What did matter was that they should
be measurable and repeatable, and that no other hypothesis
except the operation of ESP could explain the phenomena.

Previous studies of ESP had used playing cards, numbers, or
hidden objects as target material. Rhine and his colleagues
realized that this was unsatisfactory, for people have favorite

**Above: the Amazing Randi, an
American showman, with a
pack of ESP cards. He claims
to be able to duplicate psychic
feats with a combination of
sleight-of-hand, psychology,
and theatrical gimmicks. Randi
says matter-of-factly that he
can do everything that Uri Geller
has been seen to do, and also
claims that there is nothing
paranormal about any of it.**

cards and numbers, and objects are loaded with associations for them. So new target material was developed using five relatively neutral symbols: a circle, a cross, three wavy lines, a square, and a star. A deck of ESP cards (sometimes called Zener cards because Dr. Zener suggested the symbols) consists of 25 cards, five of each symbol. In making a "run" through a pack, trying to guess each card or to identify it by extrasensory perception as it is separated from the rest, a subject might be expected to score five hits purely by chance. That is, over a series of runs through the deck, his average score would, according to the laws of chance, be five. If he consistently scores more than five hits through a long series of runs it is scientifically valid to assume that some factor other than chance is at work. Of course, the extra-chance factor may be some form of cheating, or collusion with the experimenter, or it may be due to some fault in the design of the experiment or to the subject's receiving and interpreting cues in a manner that neither he nor the experimenter is consciously aware of. But if these possibilities are adequately guarded against, and the subject continues to score significantly above chance expectation, it is scientifically legitimate to claim that ESP has been demonstrated to work.

In his controversial book *Extra-Sensory Perception* Rhine reported on the work done at Duke with eight subjects who consistently scored significantly above chance in card guessing trials. Of these the star performer was Hubert Pearce, a young student in the School of Religion at Duke.

Rhine's way of conducting his experiments—for which he was later severely criticized—was to start off informally with the subject, sometimes over a cup of coffee, and gradually to increase the controls. In his work with Pearce, Rhine found that the student usually took a while to adjust to the stricter conditions, but after a brief period of low scoring he would do as well, and sometimes even better, than before. His average score in 600 runs through the 25-card pack was slightly over nine hits per run. These results, said Rhine, "are positively breath-taking when one calculates their mathematical significance." The odds against chance accounting for such results, he added are "enormous beyond our capacity to appreciate."

Most of the work with Pearce tested clairvoyance. The experimenter did not look at the cards, so if Pearce was getting the information by extrasensory means, he was getting it from the cards themselves, and not telepathically from the mind of the experimenter. There is, however, another interpretation: that Pearce's high scores were due to precognition—that he was foreseeing the correct answers that would be revealed when the experimenter checked the cards.

In some of the early trials, Pearce and the experimenter—usually Rhine or his main assistant Dr. Pratt—would sit facing each other at a table. Pearce would shuffle the pack of cards, and the experimenter would cut the pack and place it between them. Pearce would call the top card and remove it from the pack still face down. The experimenter would record the calls and then check them against the pack.

Rhine soon discovered that Pearce could not only deliberately hit the target on an average of nearly 10 tries out of 25, but he

Above: Dr. J. B. Rhine, the American parapsychologist who set himself the job of creating repeatable and statistically measurable experiments on ESP.

Right: the five Zener cards developed by Rhine's associate Dr. K. E. Zener during the 1930s. They are still used as a reliable, standard testing unit around the world. Five correct guesses out of 25 cards can be expected to be made by chance alone; more than that may be significant of possible psychic powers.

could also deliberately miss it. In a series of 225 runs Pearce averaged less than two hits per run when he was instructed to make wrong calls. He could alternate high-scoring and low-scoring runs apparently by choice. But the most amazing discovery of these early trials with Pearce was that he could guess down through the pack without a single card being moved. Rhine would place a freshly opened and thoroughly shuffled pack of cards on the table. Pearce would concentrate and write down the order in which he thought the cards were arranged down through the pack. When the results of 65 such runs through the pack were tabulated, Pearce's score was an average of 7.4 hits—significantly above chance level. In one run, urged on by Rhine's offering him $100 for each hit he got in sequence, Pearce got all 25 cards right. He didn't get the $2500, though, for Rhine said the offer was understood to be "only a figurative one."

To test Pearce's powers of clairvoyance under stricter conditions, Rhine arranged a series of experiments at long distance. After synchronizing their watches, Pearce and the experimenter, Dr. Pratt, went into separate buildings on the Duke University campus. (At first they used buildings that were 100 yards apart; later the distance was increased to 250 yards). At a prearranged time, Pratt shuffled and cut a pack of cards, placed them face down on the table in front of him, then removed the top card and put it aside without looking at it. Pearce, in the other building, had a minute in which to write down his guess for that card. Then a second card was removed, and so on through the pack. At the end of the run Pratt made a record of the sequence, then shuffled the pack and ran through the procedure again. When two runs had been completed, Pearce and Pratt sealed up their record sheets and delivered them independently to Dr. Rhine. The results of these experiments were even more impressive than many of Pearce's trials at close range. After excluding the first three runs as an "adjustment phase," Rhine found that over nearly 300 runs at 100 yards Pearce was averaging 11.4 hits per run.

Pearce was just one of the eight people Rhine discovered among the faculty and students of Duke University who possessed extraordinary ESP ability. When he published *Extra-Sensory Perception* in 1934 he was convinced that he had demonstrated by unimpeachable scientific method that ESP occurs, and had presented a case that the scientific community as a whole must pay attention to, However, the scientific community remained skeptical for the most part, and in the ensuing controversy both Rhine's experimental methods and his statistical analysis of the results were criticized. Some of his critics even questioned his integrity.

One of the skeptics was Professor Bernard Riess of Hunter College in New York City. But unlike most other critics Professor Riess decided to test the ESP hypothesis by carrying out some experiments of his own. He discovered a promising subject, a young woman who lived near him in White Plains. Following the procedure used in the Pratt-Pearce experiments at Duke, he completed a series of 74 runs over a period of several months. At a prearranged time on certain evenings Professor Riess, sitting in his study, would go through a pack of cards while the girl, a

Left: Hubert Pearce in a test with Dr. Rhine. He names cards before turning them over as Rhine records his calls. Pearce regularly scored well above chance, but suddenly lost his power at a time of great emotional stress.

Left: Duke University buildings used for "distance tests" of ESP. One series of tests was made with the subject and the experimenter in separate buildings B and C, 100 yards apart; a later series used buildings A and C, which were separated by 250 yards.

Right: the scorecard from the first distant test with Pearce. The correct calls are circled. Five correct calls are predictable by chance. Pearce's results in six series of calls are, with one exception, at least twice that.

quarter of a mile away, would write down the order of the cards. At the conclusion of the series she was discovered to have averaged the astonishing score of 18 hits per run. "Heaven knows there is no room for such results in my scientific philosophy!" Riess told a colleague. But with admirable scientific objectivity he accepted an invitation to publish a report on his experiments in the *Journal of Parapsychology*.

This is the best-ever record of success in ESP trials, but as it was not obtained under laboratory conditions and with qualified witnesses it remains on the level of anecdotal evidence. Like all other spectacularly high scorers in card guessing tests, the subject suddenly lost her powers. She underwent an illness, and when she recovered and was tested again her scores were not significantly above chance expectation. The same had happened to Hubert Pearce, who had suddenly lost his ability apparently as a consequence of receiving bad news from home.

Parapsychologists are to this day puzzled by this tendency for ESP to manifest itself spectacularly but briefly in some people. However, the very fact that once-successful subjects eventually begin to fail is one indication that the original positive results were genuine.

One researcher who was highly skeptical when he read Rhine's report of the early work at Duke was the same Dr. Soal who later established—ingeniously if eccentrically—that the stage telepathist Frederick Marion possessed no paranormal powers. Soal's skepticism was not that of the hard-line materialist. Back in the 1920s he had already shown an interest in psychical phenomena. Soal was skeptical about Rhine's work because he found it difficult to believe that over a short period of time and in one place Rhine had discovered as many as eight high-scoring subjects. He had conducted similar experiments himself and had failed to discover even one gifted subject. For several years

Above: the Duke distant ESP tests were generally conducted by having the sender in a room in one building concentrate on the card to be identified by the subject in another building.

Below: the subject who is being tested records her impression of the card the sender is holding. The stopwatches are used to synchronize action between the two.

ESP RECORD SHEET

No. _____

Subject _H. Pearce_ Experiment _Subseries D (copy)_
Observer _J.G.P. & J.B.R._ Date _Mar. 12-13, '34_
Type of Test _Clairvoyance BT_ Time _____
General conditions _Distance test — 100 yards_

Use other side for remarks. Total score _____ Avge. score _____
With ESP cards use ∧ for star, o for circle, L for square, + for cross, = for waves.

1		2		3		4		5		6		7		8		9		10	
Call	Card	Call	Card	Call	Card	Call	Card	Call	Card	Call	Card	Call	Card	Call	Card	Call	Card	Call	Card
∧	∧	o	L	o	=	+	+	o	=	L	L								
o	L	L	∧	=	o	∧	L	∧	∧	∧	+								
o	L	∧	L	∧	∧	o	o	L	=	L	o								
=	=	L	o	+	o	L	o	∧	∧	∧	∧								
+	∧	+	∧	=	+	+	+	+	=	+	L								
=	L	∧	=	o	=	L	+	=	∧	o	o								
L	L	=	=	L	L	o	o	+	+	+	L								
L	o	=	+	∧	o	+	∧	+	+	∧	=								
∧	o	o	=	L	L	o	=	o	o	+	+								
o	o	∧	+	L	∧	∧	L	+	L	+	o								
+	+	L	+	o	o	=	∧	o	=	=	∧								
+	=	o	+	+	+	+	+	+	+	o	o								
L	L	+	=	L	L	o	L	L	+	=	=								
o	∧	L	o	+	=	=	=	o	o	o	+								
∧	∧	=	L	=	+	o	∧	∧	o	∧	∧								
L	o	o	∧	L	=	∧	o	o	o	L	+								
o	=	=	o	∧	L	∧	∧	∧	=	o	L								
=	=	∧	o	+	=	=	=	=	L	+	∧								
o	+	∧	∧	L	o	o	L	=	+	=	∧								
+	+	+	o	∧	∧	+	+	L	L	o	o								
∧	∧	L	=	=	∧	o	L	=	∧	∧	=								
+	+	+	+	L	L	+	o	∧	L	+	L								
=	=	=	∧	∧	+	∧	∧	L	=	=	=								
L	o	+	L	∧	∧	=	=	+	o	+	+								
=	+	o	L	+	+	+	=	+	∧	o	=								
12	**3**	**10**		**11**		**10**		**10**											

77

after Rhine's book was published he worked diligently with numerous subjects but still failed to get any results significantly above chance expectation. When the well-known photographer Basil Shackleton walked into his office one gloomy February afternoon in 1936 and volunteered as a subject, Soal had no reason to suspect that these experiments would yield one of the strangest discoveries of ESP research.

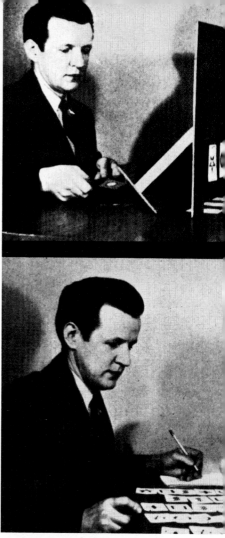

He still had no reason to suspect it after his first experimental session with Shackleton. The photographer had shown remarkable confidence when he volunteered. "I have come," he had declared, "not to be tested, but to demonstrate telepathy," and he claimed that with friends at home he could guess through a pack of playing cards from top to bottom and get most of them right. But he was disappointed in the results he produced under Soal's experimental conditions. His scores in six successive runs with the 25-card pack were 10, 7, 7, 6, 6, and 3 hits. He went away somewhat chastened, saying that he needed to have a drink or two before he could get his ESP functioning. But later, when Soal provided the "drink or two" and conditions in which Shackleton thought he could function effectively, the subject only averaged 4.1 hits per 25—well below chance expectation. A series of trials was completed, and at the end of it Soal filed away the unremarkable record of 165 hits out of 800 attempts. He forgot about Shackleton.

Three years later, Soal was persuaded to take another look at his records of the Shackleton experiments. The Cambridge psychical researcher Whately Carington had conducted some telepathy experiments himself, using pictures. On ten successive evenings he would draw a picture and hang it in a locked room in his house. His subjects, some of whom were on the other side of the Atlantic, would attempt to identify the picture by ESP and mail in their own drawings. Quite a number of these drawings, Carington noticed, matched well with a picture in his target series, but not the one which was the target for the particular evening on which they were drawn. Many of them were uncannily accurate matches with the *next* picture in the series, or with one used as the target drawing on the previous night. The delayed hits were odd enough, but the advance hits indicated that precognition might be at work. At the time the subjects made these drawings the target drawing had not even been made. In some cases, Carington had not even thought of what he would draw.

Carington termed these advanced and delayed hits a "displacement effect," and he drew Soal's attention to it. He urged Soal to look through some of the records of his old experiments to see if further evidence of this displacement effect might be found. Soal followed his suggestion—though not very optimistically or enthusiastically, for it involved a considerable amount of work. But when he checked Shackleton's scores his perseverance was at last rewarded. He discovered that this subject, whose attempts at identifying the target card had barely come up to chance expectation, had called either the one before or the one after it in the series with remarkable frequency. When Soal mathematically analyzed the results he found that the odds against their being obtained by chance were more than 2500

Top and above: another technique of card identification is the Screened Touch Matching test devised by Dr. J. G. Pratt. In this test the experimenter holds the card behind a screen, and the subject touches the symbol she believes is on that card. The experimenter then puts the card face down in the row leading from that symbol. Scoring is a simple business of counting the correct guesses of the subject.

Above right: a later example of the Screened Touch Matching Test as it has been developed from the original Duke University technique.

Left: a hand-operated mechanical shuffling machine designed to guarantee that the order of cards in a test is completely random.

to one. Shackleton's confidence in his powers of ESP had not been mistaken. He was like a marksman with a quirky bias to hit persistently just to the left or to the right of the bullseye.

Soal got in touch with Shackleton and in 1940 began a new series of experiments with him, using several different agents. He consistently scored one ahead of the target when his guesses were spaced at intervals of about 2.8 seconds, but when Soal speeded up the rate to approximately half the interval, he scored with equal consistency *two* ahead. Shackleton's ability to guess in advance in this way suggested precognition—the ability to foresee the future. Soal noted, however, that the results might also be explained by clairvoyance. Perhaps the subject was not foreseeing what would be in the agent's mind a few moments later, but psychically looking into the unturned cards as they lay on the table at that moment. As in Pearce's case, Shackleton's high scores might be attributed either to clairvoyance or to precognition.

Shackleton also improved his ability to identify the immediate target card. Once Soal asked him to prepare himself for a session the following week when he would be scored only on the target card. Shackleton gave 76 correct calls in 200 trials, a score with odds against chance of more than 10 million to one. He also responded impressively when Soal secretly introduced another

Above: S. G. Soal, mathematician and psychical researcher. Before he began his statistical work on psychic phenomena he spent some time investigating mediums, among them Mrs. Blanche Cooper. During seances with her, Soal received long and detailed messages from his friend Gordon Davis—only to learn later that Davis was still very much alive. However, Blanche Cooper had been able to foresee where Davis would be living nearly a year before he had moved there.

variation. Instead of a random arrangement of the five symbols, Soal used a pack consisting of only two symbols—12 of one symbol followed by 13 of the other. Shackleton's ESP was not thrown by this innovation. In three such nonrandom sequences introduced without warning in a series of normal random sequences, he scored 7, 12, and 13 direct hits.

When the distinguished Cambridge philosopher C. D. Broad studied the Soal-Shackleton experiments, he declared: "There can be no doubt that the events described happened and were correctly reported; that the odds against chance coincidence piled up to billions to one; and that the nature of the events which involved both telepathy and precognition, conflicts with one or more of the basic limiting principles [of science and common sense]."

Another Cambridge philosopher, Professor R. H. Thouless (who coined the umbrella-term psi) wrote in 1942: "The reality of the phenomena [of ESP] must be regarded as proved as certainly as anything in scientific research can be proved . . . Let us now give up the task of trying to prove again to the satisfaction of the skeptical that the psi effect really exists, and try instead to devote ourselves to the task of finding out all we can about it."

A great deal had in fact already been found out about ESP in the 12 years between the beginning of Rhine's work at Duke University and the time Professor Thouless wrote these words. But it was a puzzling body of knowledge, little more than a series of glimpses of a still mysterious paranormal faculty. This faculty could be demonstrated to work, and in some cases to work in obedience to certain laws, but it showed no overall pattern or lawfulness in its occurrence. Professor Thouless was right to emphasize that much remained to be discovered about the nature of ESP, and that it was a waste of time to persist with research designed to prove its already proven existence.

What precisely had been found out about psi up to this time?

First, it had been demonstrated independently by researchers in different countries that in card guessing tests some people can show a consistent record of success that rules out chance as an explanation, and that can only be explained as the operation of ESP.

This ability seemed to be rare and short-lived. Consistently high scorers were difficult to find, and even they often lost their ability suddenly.

ESP, however, was not entirely an involuntary process. Gifted guessers like Pearce or Shackleton seemed able to score high or low, directly on the target card or on one of its neighbors, at will.

ESP was seen to operate most effectively when the subject was relaxed, and free from distractions. It could be temporarily destroyed by a depressant drug, such as sodium amytal, and restored (but not improved) by a stimulant, such as caffeine. In tests for telepathy, it tended to vary according to the relationship between the subject and the agent.

In the early days of research it had been assumed that telepathy was the most plausible form of ESP because it was easier to conceive of mind reacting with mind than of mind reacting with matter or transcending the limitations of time. But the discovery of Pearce's ability to guess down through the pack, and of the displacement effect in Carington's and Soal's researches, cast some doubt on this assumption. Some parapsychologists began to wonder if clairvoyance and precognition were perhaps more common than telepathy.

Such ambiguities in experimental results induced researchers to design some very careful and ingenious experiments, in which only one kind of ESP—telepathy, clairvoyance, or precognition—was tested and the others excluded.

ESP appeared to work equally effectively at any distance. This ruled out the possibility of its being explained in terms of any known physical law, for at that time all physical forces were believed to decline, however slightly, with the distance traveled. Although recently some exceptions to that rule have been discovered, we still don't know how ESP functions. We see only the results of its functioning.

The results themselves are fairly exciting even today—decades after Rhine reported his first experiments with Pearce. And although star subjects like Pearce are rare, some researchers now believe that everyone may possess ESP to some degree. Readers who would like to explore the possibility of ESP in themselves or their friends can easily set up their own simple experiments. This can be undertaken in the spirit of a game, but if it is properly conducted it could produce a valid contribution to current ESP research. The characteristics of the ESP faculty are by no means fully understood today, and any parapsychologist would be delighted to hear of the discovery of another consistently high-scoring subject like Hubert Pearce or Basil Shackleton.

Because the ESP faculty functions best when the subject is relaxed and uninhibited, it is a good idea to follow Rhine's approach of starting off informally and not making too much fuss over techniques and precautions. If a subject shows high-scoring ability the controls and conditions can be tightened up as the experimental series progresses. Initially, it is essential only to insure that the subject cannot obtain normal sensory information about the target cards. If he can see the backs of the cards, make sure there are no distinguishing marks on them. Also make sure there are no reflecting surfaces in the room that might enable him to glimpse the faces of the cards.

Preliminary experiments might be conducted with the subject and agent sitting at opposite ends of a five- or six-foot long

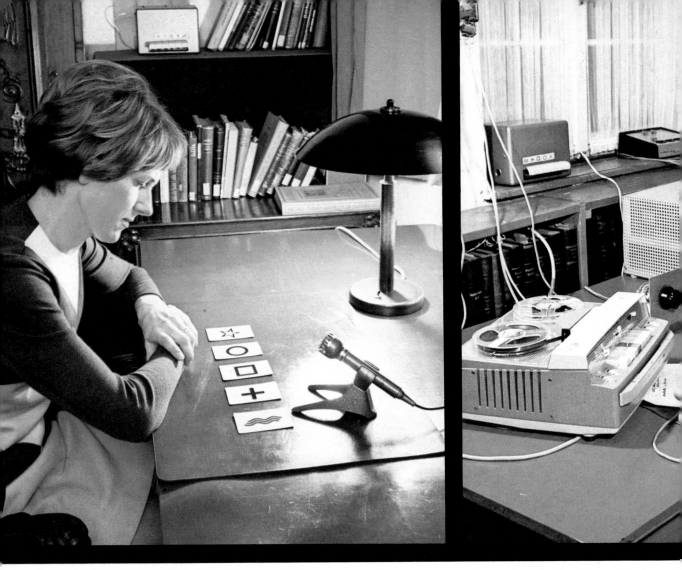

table which was fitted with an improvised screen in the middle.

Zener cards are manufactured and sold commercially. The authorized distributor is Haines House of Cards, Norwalk, Ohio. Detailed instructions accompanying the pack explain how to test for clairvoyance and telepathy in several different ways.

Another kind of test can be constructed following a method adapted from one devised by S. G. Soal. Materials needed include five ordinary playing cards—the ace through the five—and five picture cards. Soal used cards with colored pictures of five animals: an elephant, a giraffe, a lion, a penguin, and a zebra. The idea was that animals were more easily visualized than the abstract Zener symbols, and so might be more effective in pure telepathy tests. Cards bearing these symbols can easily be improvised or, alternatively, other picture cards may be used. Ideally, the names of the symbols should begin with different letters so that the subject need write only one letter for each trial.

Three people are required for this telepathy test: the subject, the agent, and the experimenter. The subject and the agent sit at opposite ends of the table with the screen between them, and the experimenter sits at the side of the table at the agent's end. The experimenter holds the five playing cards. The agent has the five

Above: a distant ESP test at the Freiburg Institut in Germany conducted by Dr. Hans Bender. The receiver (at left) is two rooms away from the sender (at right). The sender tries to transmit his choice to the receiver, first letting the control room (center) know what it is, and then signaling the receiver to make her choice. The sender's choices are tape recorded, and the controller keeps a record of the calls from the receiver. This particular experiment had a high success rate—681 hits out of 2770 calls. The expected rate of success by chance would be 554 hits.

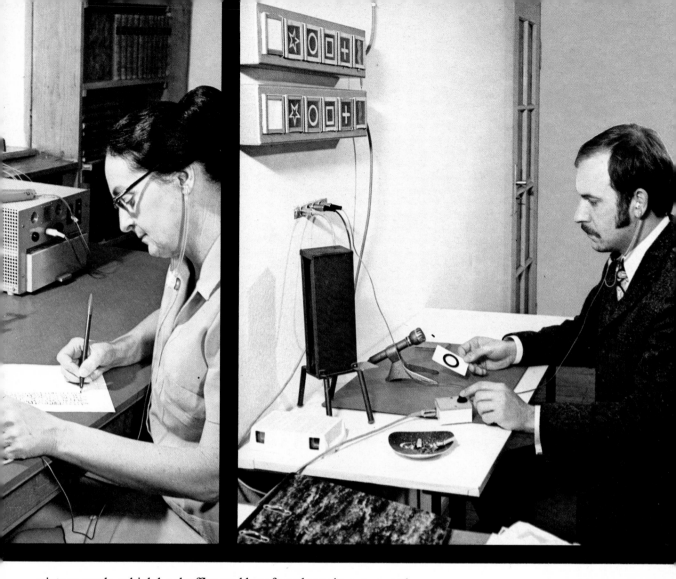

picture cards, which he shuffles and lays face down in a row on the table in front of him. As an extra precaution they may be laid out in a cardboard box turned on its side, thus screening them from both the subject and the experimenter.

Both the experimenter and the subject have scoring sheets in front of them with lines numbered 1 to 25. To begin, the experimenter shuffles his five playing cards and shows one selected at random to the agent, saying as he does so, "one." This signals the subject to be ready to make his first guess. The experimenter then writes the number of the playing card on his scoring sheet and reshuffles the five cards. Meanwhile, the agent notes the number of the playing card shown to him, and looks at the face of the appropriate picture card in front of him. If it was a 3, for example, he will look at the third card from the left. The subject writes against the number 1 on his scoring sheet the initial letter (E, G, L, P, or Z if the animals pictures are used) of his guess at the target picture.

When a run of 25 guesses has been completed, the agent shows the experimenter the order of the target pictures. The experimenter can then assign the letters E, G, L, P, or Z to the corresponding numbers of the playing cards on his scoring sheet.

The target cards are then reshuffled and laid out in a different order in preparation for another run. When the desired number of runs have been completed, the letters on the subject's scoring sheet are compared with the actual sequences on the experimenter's sheet.

The experiment can be converted into one testing clairvoyance if the agent does *not* look at the face of each picture card as its number is shown.

If private ESP experimentation is entered into seriously, it must be continued over several sessions and several hundred individual trials, or guesses. Rhine has said that most of his good subjects did not do particularly well in their first hundred trials.

To do well means to score consistently and significantly above the chance expectation of five hits per run of 25 guesses. On a series of 100 or more runs an average of even six or seven is significant. It would be premature to take it as signifying the operation of ESP, however. The high score might indicate a fault in the procedure. This would be the stage to introduce stricter controls and conditions.

The Soal-Shackleton experiments were conducted with the subject and agent in separate rooms with the door open so that

Right: another method of testing ESP. At a signal a person behind a curtain tries to guess the one of 25 squares chosen. His choices are recorded by the experimenter sitting on the right.

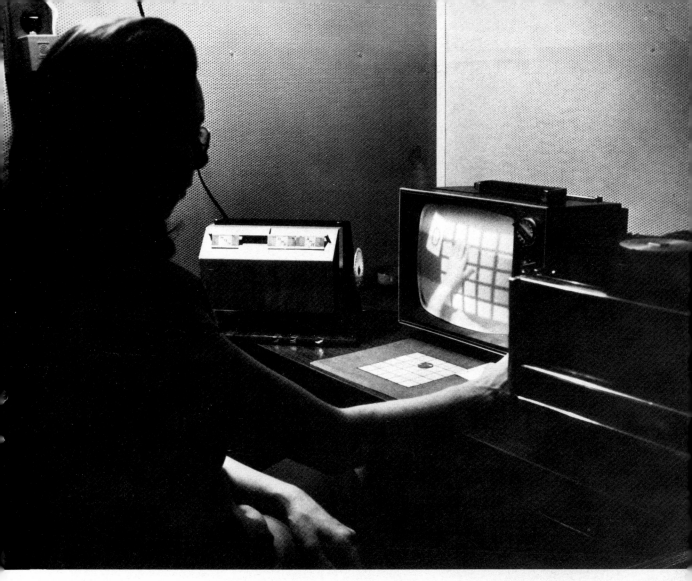

Above: in another room the sender
concentrates on a TV picture
of the receiver's hand moving
over the squares, and tries to
influence the choice by telepathy.
The sender in this experiment
was Janet Mitchell, a well-known
American psychical researcher.

the subject could hear the experimenter's cue-calls for the synchronization of his guesses. This is one improvement that could be introduced with a successful scorer after the preliminary trials. Another is to insure randomness in the numbers turned up by the experimenter. It is possible that in shuffling his five cards and picking one out for each guess he might, consciously or unconsciously, choose them in a certain order. This order might be picked up by the subject or it might correspond to an order that he favors. To eliminate this possibility the experimenter can prepare in advance lists of 25 random numbers, which he then communicates in sequence to the agent by holding up the corresponding playing cards. Such lists can be compiled from tables of logarithms or from a telephone directory, using the last digits of numbers down a column in the sequence in which they occur, and of course ignoring all digits except those falling into the range 1 to 5.

If, when these extra precautions have been taken, your subject continues to average seven or more hits per run over a long series of trials, you may have reason to suspect a serious case of supernormality—and should lose no time in calling in your nearest parapsychologist.

Mind Over Matter

Can thought alone make physical objects move? The idea has been a fascinating one for many psychical researchers, especially because there is a long history of well-documented reports of objects moving mysteriously with no apparent natural cause. Right: Polish medium Stanislawa Tomczyt during an experiment with Schrenck-Notzing. She seems to have succeeded in suspending a pair of scissors in the air.

On January 14, 1966, the Miami police were asked to investigate some strange occurrences at a warehouse owned by Tropication Arts, Inc., a company that dealt in novelty items and souvenirs for the tourist trade. The complaint clerk at the station told Patrolman William Killam: "This person who called said he had a ghost in his place of business . . . going around breaking ashtrays, and he said they were just coming up off the floor and breaking." Patrolman Killam went off on his assignment muttering something about being sent to deal with "a lot of nuts."

When he arrived at the warehouse the

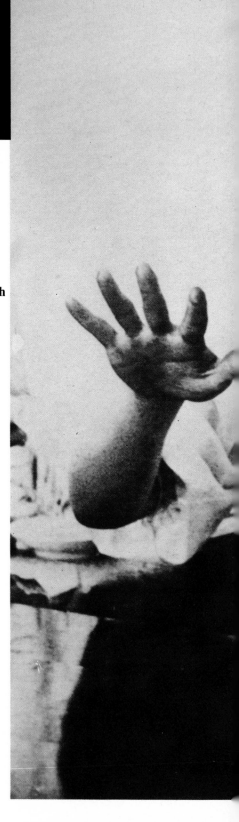

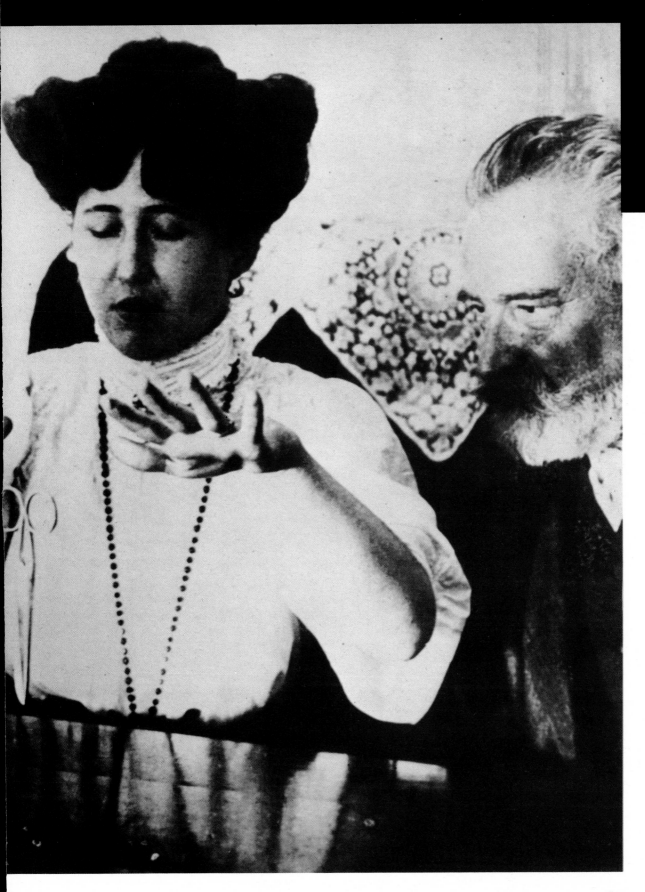

"Killam...saw something that stopped him in his tracks..."

owner told him that the breakages had started about a month earlier. At first he had put it down to carelessness on the part of the staff, but as weeks went by and the rate of breakage increased he realized that something very peculiar and unnatural was going on. Patrolman Killam listened skeptically, then said he'd better take a look around the warehouse. He walked along the aisles, sometimes stopping to stamp on the floor or shake one of the shelves in order to see if this would dislodge anything. Everything seemed normal and secure. Killam had walked the length of three aisles and was beginning to walk down a fourth when he saw something that stopped him in his tracks. A highball glass that was standing among others on a shelf suddenly rose into the air, traveled a few feet, and smashed onto the floor. Nobody else was near the spot, and when Killam shook the shelf roughly none of the other glasses moved.

Clearly this problem was beyond the capacity of the police. Psychical investigators were called in. They were Dr. J. G. Pratt of the Parapsychology Laboratory at Duke University, and Dr. W. G. Roll of the Psychical Research Foundation. Since their investigation of the "Seaford Poltergeist" that had tormented a Long Island family in 1958, they had become a kind of flying squad for the investigation of reported poltergeist phenomena. With a team of helpers they spent some weeks at the Tropication Arts warehouse, recording every incident in great detail, analyzing them, and looking for a common factor that would explain them. In all they recorded 224 incidents, 78 of which they themselves witnessed. The common factor turned out to be a 19-year-old employee, Cuban refugee Julio Vasquez. In most of the records of poltergeist happenings collected over the years there commonly is a mention of the presence of a young person, usually one who is going through some kind of emotional crisis. So the investigators had known what to look for. But their detailed recording of the incidents in this case yielded some interesting new discoveries.

The breakages had all occurred when Julio was in the warehouse, but not always when he was near the objects. Moreover, they nearly all occurred when he had his back toward the object that was moved, and the movements took place on his left side, never on his right. When the movements of the objects were plotted and the distances they traveled were measured, it was found that, as they had moved away from Julio, they had not traveled in a straight line but in a curve. Analysis of the distances the objects traveled in relation to their distance from Julio at the time of the incident revealed a precise mathematical ratio. This was found to agree with what is known in physics as the "law of exponential decay." This is the law that describes the weakening effect in many natural processes—for example, bacterial and radioactive decay, and the conversion of light to heat energy as it penetrates water. After studying and interpreting all the data, the investigators reached a conclusion: contrary to the warehouse owners' suspicions, no ghosts were involved. Julio was the poltergeist. The energy that caused the smashing of objects came from him.

The German word *poltergeist* translates as "boisterous or noisy spirit." But modern psychical researchers have come to

Photographic reconstructions of poltergeist activities that afflicted the Plach family of Vachendorf. Their teenage daughter may have caused them. Objects disappeared and reappeared, stones and coals flew through the air, and tools somehow escaped from a trunk on which Mrs. Plach was sitting. Left: Mr. Plach watches things flying around through the air. Below left: plates of food spilled. Below: Professor Hans Bender, who investigated the case in 1948, with Mrs. Plach. She kept a careful diary recording all the peculiar manifestations. Bottom: Mrs. Plach working on her diary as something flies past.

the conclusion that poltergeist phenomena have nothing to do with spirits. Instead they are believed to be involuntary PK effects. They are caused by the release of pent-up psychic energy. The mystery remaining is how this psychic energy gets converted to kinetic energy, capable of moving matter.

For most people, PK is a more difficult concept to come to terms with than ESP. It is difficult enough to accept that mind can interact with mind without any apparent channel of communication, but to propose that mind can interact with matter is even more implausible. Yet today the idea of psychosomatic illnesses and psychic healing, which most of the medical profession would have scoffed at not so long ago, is widely accepted. It is not so generally realized that these medical phenomena involve a mind-matter interaction that no known laws can explain. Still, the skeptic could point out that psychosomatic illness and psychic healing involve interaction between mind and matter in the same body. What is implausible is that mind can act upon matter outside the body, that a person can influence events in the external material world by pure will.

One day early in 1934 a young man walked into Dr. J. B. Rhine's office at Duke University and announced, "Hey, doc, I've got something to tell you I think you ought to know." He was, he explained, a professional gambler, and it was his experience that when he was in a certain state of mind, which he described as "hot," he could influence the dice to come up as he wanted them to by exercising his will. He had heard about Dr. Rhine's ESP research and thought that Rhine would be the man to take his discovery seriously and investigate it scientifically. He was right. Within minutes Dr. Rhine and the gambler were crouched on the floor in a corner of the office rolling dice.

Thus begun a long experimental program of PK research at Duke, the results of which were not published until 10 years later. Rhine and his colleagues had had enough trouble getting the scientific community to accept their evidence for ESP, and they didn't want to complicate the controversy prematurely by claiming to be able to demonstrate PK in the laboratory as well. So for nine years, the dice-rolling experiments continued quietly at Duke, and the results were carefully recorded and analyzed but not published.

The advantage of using dice in PK experiments is the same as the advantage of using cards to test ESP—the results can be statistically analyzed and an odds-against-chance calculation can be made. When two dice ("die" in the singular) are thrown together the sum of the faces can range from 2 to 12. There are 36 combinations of the two dice, 15 of which add up to values of 8 or more and 15 others to values of 6 or less, while 6 combinations produce the sum of 7. The two dice must be distinguishable from each other to produce this variety of results. For example, a three on die "a" and a four on die "b" can thus count as a separate score to a four on "a" and a three on "b", even though the numbers are the same in both cases.

The target in a PK test can be high scores, low scores, or sevens. Alternatively, a particular number can be made the target. At the end of a run, which at Duke was arbitrarily set as either 24 throws of separate dice, or 12 throws of pairs, or 8 throws of three dice, the deviation from chance expectation can be precisely calculated. The experimenter found that the most convenient procedure was to throw a pair of dice 12 times, and to will either high or low combinations to come up. The chance expectation for either result is five hits per run. This figure is arrived at by dividing the number of low or high combinations— which is 15 each—by 3, which is the number of times that 12, the number of throws, goes into 36, the number of possible combinations. In other words, the chances of a hit are reduced *in proportion* to the number of attempts. If there were 36 throws in a run, the chance of a hit would rise proportionately to 15. Of course, all such calculations of chance are based on a large number of runs. In the short term, results might deviate

Below: a mechanical dice tumbler devised by the Duke Parapsychology Laboratory and still in use today. The dice are at the bottom of the set-up, on the right side.

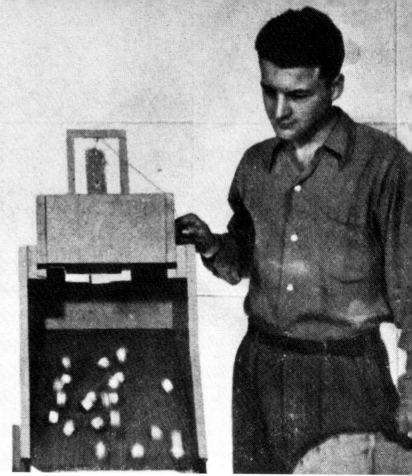

Above: in one of the PK tests devised by Dr. Betty M. Humphrey at Duke, 24 dice are used at once.

Right: in another Humphrey test, the two subjects engage in a "tug of wills" experiment. Each of them wills a different side of the dice to appear uppermost.

sharply from chance expectation without implying that factors other than chance are at work.

The first series of recorded experiments conducted at Duke consisted of 562 runs. There were 3110 hits, whereas the chance expectation was 2810 hits (5 times 562). So there were 300 more hits than pure chance would have produced. Calculations based upon probability theory showed that this result would not come up more than once in a billion times by chance alone.

After this encouraging exploratory stage the researchers at Duke felt it was time to vary and tighten up the conditions of the experiments in order to see if the results could be attributed to any cause other than PK. Two possible other causes were the employment of skill by the thrower of the dice, and the existence of a physical bias in the dice themselves. Dice on which the marker spots are hollowed out may slightly favor the higher numbers because their faces have had more material removed and are therefore fractionally lighter than the faces of the lower numbers. To rule out skill as a factor in throwing, the experimenters used various throwing devices, such as a chute with a corrugated surface and an electrically operated release mechanism. To prevent bias in the dice influencing the results, they used special precision-made dice. Also the targets within series of runs were systematically alternated so that the effect of any bias would be canceled out. Many more experiments were conducted under such improved conditions at Duke and elsewhere, and results significantly above chance were continually obtained. Unlike the ESP experiments, however, this research revealed no

Below: one of the Duke subjects trying PK tests after having been given a narcotic, sodium amytal, which made her very drowsy but didn't put her to sleep. The investigators found that large doses lowered the scoring rate. In contrast, small doses seemed to be followed by a rise in the subject's scoring.

spectacularly high-scoring subjects. The work suggested that PK was a latent faculty that many, if not most people possessed, but that it rarely manifested itself as more highly developed in one subject than in another.

One of the most positive results in these trials was obtained in an amusing experiment that took the form of a contest between divinity students and gamblers. A student at the Duke Divinity School conceived the idea that PK might be an operating factor in cases of prayer apparently influencing events in the physical world. He put his idea to Rhine, who suggested that, because the divinity students would be highly motivated to succeed in order to demonstrate the efficacy of prayer, it might be interesting to compare their results with those of another group of strongly motivated individuals. So four young men noted for their success in crap shooting were found and matched against four prospective ministers. After a total of 1242 runs of a type in which the chance expectancy average was 4.00 hits per run, the gamblers had obtained an average run score of 4.52 and the divinity students an average of 4.51. This was virtually a tie. The interesting result of the experiment, though, was that when the results of both groups were combined and statistically analyzed, they were found to be likely to occur by chance only once in billions of tests. It was clear that motivation was a potent influence in PK trials, whether that motivation was religious or otherwise.

The most conclusive evidence for the operation of PK in the Duke experiments did not emerge in the course of the experiments themselves but later, when the results were analyzed. In 1943 active research at Duke was at a standstill because of the war, so Rhine and his only remaining research assistant dug out the results of all the dice-rolling experiments of the previous nine years and had another look at them. They found a sharp drop in the above-chance scores from the first run in a test to the later runs. The experimenters had noted such declines at the time of making the tests, but had paid little attention to them. Now, when the separate tests were taken together and the overall pattern discovered to be one of a sharp drop in above-chance scoring, the scores acquired new significance. The same drop occurred in tests using mechanical dice-throwing machines, which, unlike humans, would not suffer the fatigue that often accounts for a scoring decline in many kinds of psychological tests. Reporting on the discovery of these "position effects" in the book *Mind Over Matter*, Dr. Louisa Rhine observed that they showed that PK was not just an ability sometimes to hit a target, "but a process connected with and expressed according to deep unconscious motivating factors, just as ESP had been found to be."

This delayed discovery armed the parapsychologists with a strong argument against the charge of fraud, for the evidence of the position effects had lain in the records for years without anyone suspecting it, and the patterns could not conceivably have been fraudulently introduced by the original experimenters, for no one had known at the time that such patterns would ever be significant.

When the accounts of the Duke experiments were published,

more researchers became interested in PK. W. E. Cox, an amateur, became closely associated with Duke. He was a businessman with a talent for gadgetry. He devised several dice-throwing experiments using a variety of clock mechanisms, mercury switches, electrical relays, and complicated structures built in three and five tiers with different target areas for the dice to be directed to by PK. These experiments introduced a new skill that became known as "placement PK." In this case the object was not to influence a particular face of a die to come up but to influence freely rolling dice to come to rest in a particular place.

The outstanding contribution to research in placement PK was made by Haakon Forwald, a Swedish engineer-physicist. During the early 1950s he conducted independent experiments, rolling dice down an inclined plane and trying to will them to fall either on the left or the right side of a table. In 1957 he paid a visit to Duke and joined forces with Dr. Pratt. The Pratt-Forwald experiment subsequently became widely regarded as the most successful demonstration of PK.

In this experiment six wooden cubes were released mechanically and rolled down a chute onto a horizontal surface with a dividing line down the middle. The PK task was not to direct the cubes into one of the target areas but to influence those that fell in one area to roll farther than those that fell in the other. Lines drawn on the table parallel to the center line, at intervals of one centimeter, enabled the experimenter to measure the degree of displacement of the cubes from the center. A long

series of trials produced a highly significant positive result with odds against chance of 5000 to one.

By the end of the 1950s the reality of PK was as firmly established by experimental method and statistical analysis as was that of ESP. But both ESP and PK as studied in the laboratory seemed to be relatively weak forces. PK research had only established the possibility of mental influence on small objects already in motion. Nobody had managed under laboratory conditions to make a stationary object move. Yet this is what happens in poltergeist phenomena and in some of the alleged physical effects produced by mediums in the seance room. All researchers in the field knew Professor Winther's report on the PK feats of the Danish medium Anna Rasmussen back in the 1920s, but no such talented subject had appeared on the scene since really scientific methods of control and analysis had been developed. There were, however, other areas of apparent PK activity that might repay scientific study. These included the phenomena of thought-photography, or "thoughtography," and psychic healing.

In 1910 the professor of psychology at Tokyo University, Tomokichi Fukurai, tested a woman of reported psychic ability for clairvoyance. He conceived the idea of having her identify clairvoyantly an image imprinted on a film plate which had not been developed. After the test he discovered that another plate had apparently been affected by the clairvoyant's effort at concentration. In later experiments he asked her to try to transfer specific images—usually geometrical figures or Japanese characters—onto unexposed film plates. No camera was used, and the target plate was sandwiched between the others. The woman consistently succeeded in imprinting the middle plate with the designated image, leaving the two outer plates entirely clear. Fukurai published a book on his strange discovery, and the ensuing controversy over his work on psychic phenomena forced him to resign his university position.

Little more was heard of thoughtography until the 1960s. Then a Denver psychiatrist, Dr. Jule Eisenbud, began investigating the claim of a Chicago bellhop, Ted Serios, that he could put images onto a polaroid film simply by staring into the camera lens. Eisenbud investigated Serios over several years and reported the phenomenon in numerous articles and a book entitled *The World of Ted Serios*. On various occasions, Serios produced recognizable pictures of people, cars, and buildings, such as the Denver Hilton Hotel. These are included in the book. Serios was also investigated by Dr. Pratt, who got him to spend a month at the parapsychology laboratory at the University of Virginia. Before Dr. Pratt's planned series of increasingly controlled experiments could be completed Serios—who was highly unreliable and inclined to drink—left unceremoniously. So his claims remain unproved, and the question of whether a chemical reaction can be effected on sensitized film by PK awaits further investigation.

The investigation of the psychic healer Oscar Estebany of Montreal yielded far more satisfactory and conclusive results. Estebany, a former Hungarian army colonel, discovered his healing abilities in the 1930s in the course of massaging cavalry

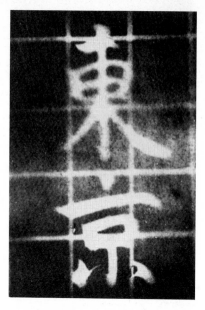

Above: one of the examples of "thoughtography" by the Japanese medium Mrs. Ikuko Nagao, from a book by Tomokichi Fukurai who investigated her powers in 1910. These characters were transfered by her to an unexposed film plate, placed in between other plates on which no image appeared.

Right: Ted Serios, who became a famous thoughtographer, tries to project a mental image through the lens of a camera held by researcher Dr. Jule Eisenbud.

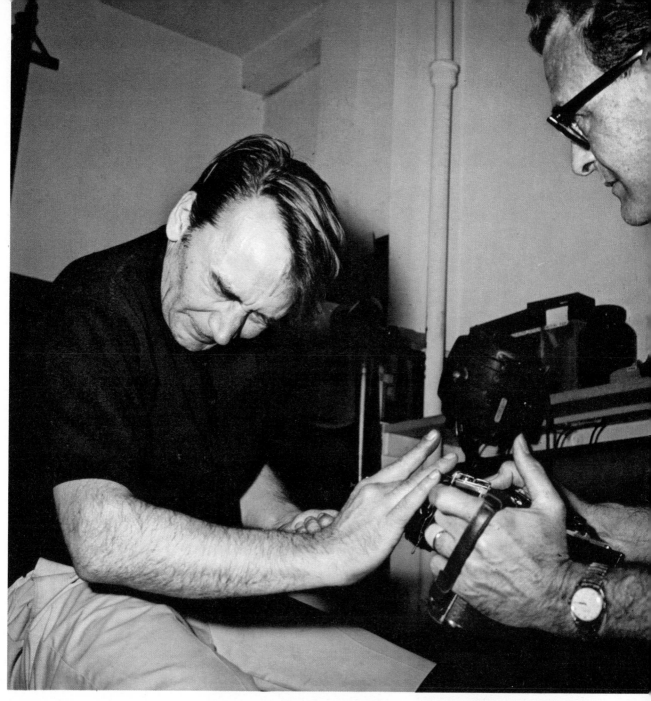

Left: a view of Rome which
Serios tried to reproduce mentally
by means of thoughtography during a test by Dr. Eisenbud. He
had seen the picture in a book.
Right: one of the images produced
by Serios, showing the dome of
the Church of Santa Maria di
Loreto. Its angle is noticeably not
the same as that of the original.
Right: another image showing
Trajan's Column. Again the angle
and pattern of shadows varies
from that of the target picture.

horses. He gained a reputation as a healer in Budapest in the 1940s, and continued to practice when he moved to Canada in the mid-1950s. Hundreds of cures, mostly of disorders that have defied the efforts of conventional medical practitioners, are attributed to him. In 1961 Estebany agreed to let Dr. Bernard Grad of McGill University test his healing power scientifically.

The obvious rational explanation of psychic healing is that it is effected by suggestion. In other words, the patient's faith in the healer effects the cure. Therefore Dr. Grad started his experiments with 300 patients that had no faith in, or knowledge of, Estebany's alleged powers. The patients were mice. Dr. Grad inflicted a small identical wound on all 300 mice, and divided them into three equal groups. The first group was treated by Estebany, the second by people who claimed no psychic healing powers, and the third was left untreated as a control group. The treatment consisted simply of the healer holding each cage of mice for 15 minutes twice a day. After 16 days the wounds were measured. It was found that those on the mice that Estebany had treated were only half the size of those on the other two groups of mice.

In another experiment Dr. Grad compared the growth of two groups of potted barley plants. One group was watered with a solution that Estebany had held for 30 minutes, and the other was watered with some of the same solution that Estebany had not tried to influence. The psychically treated water consistently promoted stronger and healthier growth in the plants than the untreated water. Dr. Grad reported his experiments in the *International Journal of Parapsychology* but he was unable to offer an explanation of the results.

Above: Dr. Justa Smith, scientist and Franciscan nun who worked with the Canadian healer Oscar Estebany to investigate whether psi powers can affect enzymes.

More searching investigations of Estebany's powers were conducted by Dr. M. Justa Smith, research director of the Human Dimensions Institute at Rosary Hill College in Buffalo, New York. Dr. Smith, a biochemist who is also a Franciscan nun, reasoned that if psychic healing works, it must work at the enzyme level in the body's cells. Enzymes are the substances that promote chemical changes in the cells, and enzyme failure is the root physical cause of disease. In order to promote health, the chemical reactions of certain enzymes within the body need to be accelerated and others to be slowed down.

Dr. Smith had done a great deal of research with the enzyme *trypsin*, which she knew can be severely damaged by exposure to ultraviolet light. She prepared a flask of trypsin in solution, damaged its molecular structure with ultraviolet light, and had Estebany hold his hands over the sides of the flask. Every 15 minutes she removed a small quantity of the solution and analyzed it in a highly sensitive machine called a *spectrophotometer*. In earlier experiments with Estebany, Dr. Smith had discovered that he could accelerate reactions in healthy enzyme chains, but now she found that he could actually repair damaged molecules. Follow-up experiments with other healers and other enzymes confirmed the discovery. The psychic healers in Dr. Smith's experiments had no way of knowing which enzymes were in solution in the flasks they held, or whether an acceleration or deceleration of activity in a particular flask would have a potentially positive effect on the

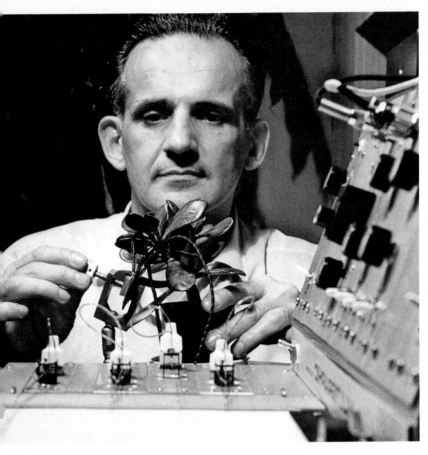

Left: animals and even micro-organisms have been used in psi research, but Cleve Backster caused a stir when he claimed that plants react to stress caused by unkind thoughts and acts of humans. Backster, a lie-detector expert, calls this phenomenon "primary perception." So far he has not been able to successfully repeat his experiments —which he has carried out since 1966—under controlled conditions.

body. Yet invariably the healers caused chemical reactions of the kind appropriate in each case. When Dr. Smith presented the results of her research to the scientific world she appropriately titled her paper *Psychic Healing: Myth into Science*.

Whether psychic healing is brought about by energies emanating from the mind of the healer or from his body is still an open question. Only if it comes from his mind could we accurately term this healing a psychokinetic function. But this is a question of terminology that need not worry us at this point. What such research as Dr. Smith's has established is that some people possess powers that are outside the ken of modern physical science, and until these powers are more fully understood, it is convenient to group them under the general idea of PK.

An experiment that demonstrated PK influence at the cellular level, without involving the complicating factors in cases of psychic healing, was made by the English researcher Nigel Richmond. Richmond tried to influence by PK the movement of *paramecia*, which are single-celled organisms about .01 inch long, found in pond water. His method was to place a drop of pond water on a microscope slide, put a paramecium in the center of the microscopic field, and try to will the organism to swim where he wanted it to. For this purpose he divided the microscopic field into four quarters using two crossed hairs, and assigned each quarter to one of the four suits of playing cards. He determined the target area each time by turning up a card from the top of a shuffled deck.

Each attempt to influence the paramecium's direction of exit lasted 15 seconds. If a paramecium swam out of the field of view before the time had elapsed, it was still counted in the scoring by being assigned to the quarter through which it had passed. In all he made 1495 attempts. Chance expectation for a paramecium hitting the target area was one-fourth of this number, or 373.75. Richmond found that the paramecia hit the target 483 times, a deviation of 109.25 over chance expectation. He also found that the creatures often went into the quarter diagonally opposite the target area. Out of the 1495 attempts, this area was hit 444 times—70.25 above chance. Richmond counted these diagonal scores as hits and grouped them with the target-hitting scores because, he wrote: "I suspect that influence applied in one direction would sometimes have its effects in the diametrically opposed direction...." Whether or not he was justified in giving equal value to these opposite scores, the fact remains that he got considerably above-chance results for his target quarters. His experiment seemed to indicate that his mind influenced the movements of other living organisms by the power of PK.

Some parapsychologists, however, have raised the question whether the results might not show telepathy at work between the experimenter and the paramecia. This suggestion sounds preposterous, for telepathy is such an astonishing power that we tend to think of it as restricted to human beings, if we believe in it at all. But many experiments, particuarly with dogs, cats, and horses, have indicated that the psi faculty—including telepathy and even PK—may not be confined to humans.

In 1970 Dr. Helmut Schmidt, now Research Director of the Mind Science Foundation, San Antonio, Texas, reported some experiments testing the PK ability of a cat. The point of the experiment was to see if the cat could manage to exert PK to turn on a lamp, by which it could warm itself, more often than the lamp would turn on by chance.

The governing mechanism for the lamp was a device called a random number generator. One of the chief problems in psi research is insuring randomness in the target materials. If one is testing for clairvoyance or for PK, it is important to eliminate the possibility of the experimenter knowing—even unconsciously—which card will turn up, for example, or which times the light will go on. If the experimenter or anyone else knows the answer, one would have to include the possibility of telepathy in any positive results. The most random known process in nature is the rate of decay of radioactive particles. In a pile of strontium atoms, for instance, half of the atoms will disintegrate over a period of 20 years. There is no way, however, of knowing which ones will disintegrate during this period, or at what time they will do so. When the disintegration takes place energy is emitted, and the random number generator uses this energy to turn on nine lights arranged in a circle, one at a time. The lights go on in a clockwise or counterclockwise direction depending on the decay rate of the strontium nuclei. The experimental subject's task is to make the lights go on in a given direction. This in turn governs the turning on and off of the generator. Success means that the subject has influenced,

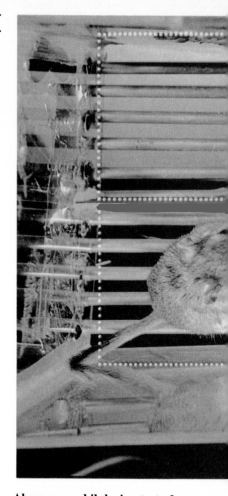

Above: a gerbil during tests for precognitive ability. Mild shocks are administered about once a minute to one half of the box, selected by a random number generator. The animal presumably guesses which side is about to be shocked and jumps to the other. In a fairly long series of tests, the results have been above those predicted by chance—indicating that even gerbils might possess some higher psi faculties.

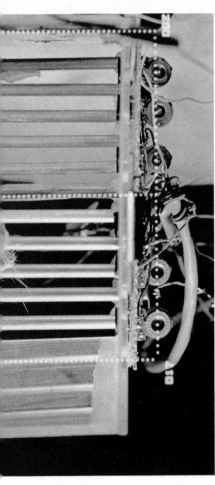

Right: Dr. Robert Morris of the Psychical Research Foundation in North Carolina conducting a test of ESP in animals. In this test, a person just outside the room tries to influence which squares the cat will move to. Dr. Morris feels that there is considerable evidence for believing that animals have psi powers. "Results with animals are at least as positive and consistent as human results," he says.

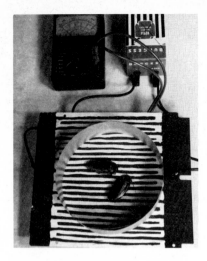

Above: cockroaches being tested for possible PK abilities in an experiment conducted by Dr. Helmut Schmidt. The insects were put on a wire grid fitted with a random number generator, and given intermittent shocks. The aim was to see if they could reduce the number of shocks by means of PK on the generator. Instead, their wild behavior produced 300 more shocks than chance would have.

presumably by PK, the behavior of subatomic particles.

The cat used in Schmidt's experiments obviously couldn't know about the subatomic particles, but it clearly had an interest in turning on the lamp that was attached to the generator. For half an hour every afternoon, the cat was put into a shack inside which the temperature was 0°C—not cold enough to cause the cat serious discomfort, but not the kind of temperature a cat likes. In one part of the shack was the 200-Watt lamp, going on and off at intervals of a few seconds or less. Every second a number was being generated that would determine whether the lamp was on or off.

For the first five experiments in the series, the cat went straight to the lamp on entering the shack, and at the end of the 30 minutes was found curled up next to it. The experimenters found that the light had been on slightly more than 50 percent of the time. More specifically, out of the 9000 numbers generated one per second during the five sessions, 4615 had turned on the lamp—115 more than the 4500 expected according to chance. These results were interesting, but not startling.

Schmidt continued the experiment for another five afternoons. It was found that the cat's behavior changed. When the door was opened at the end of the sixth session, it dashed out of the shack. In none of the remaining sessions was it found sitting by the lamp as it had at first. "It seemed to have developed a dislike for the flashing lamp," reported Schmidt. Moreover, the generator turned on by chance fewer times than expected during the second series of five sessions. Was the animal

Left: using equipment designed by Dr. Schmidt, a subject presses a button to indicate which light she thinks will flash next.

Right: in still another Schmidt experiment, lights are flashed by a random generator while the subject tries to influence the order of flashing. If she does succeed, it would apparently be only by somehow influencing the behavior of subatomic particles.

capable of exerting PK but resentful at being bullied into performing? This is a tempting conclusion for anyone who knows cats. Unfortunately, the experiment was too short to prove anything. The onset of warm weather, affecting the temperature inside the shack, forced Schmidt to discontinue the tests. Over a period of 10 days, the variation from chance in both directions was too slight to indicate with any certainty the existence of feline PK.

A significant discovery about PK that has emerged from research done so far is that it is goal-oriented. That is, when it functions, it seems to accomplish an aimed-for result directly, without the person, animal, or lower organism that exercises it having any conscious conception, so far as we can tell, of the processes that lead to this result. This is the stumbling block for the rational mind. We can possibly conceive of will as a consciously controlled operative force influencing events in the material world. But the idea of will divorced from consciousness, working on the world without any guiding idea of *how* it works, without any program, is hard to swallow. It conflicts with our understanding of natural processes as being governed by laws of cause and effect. Yet there seems no way out of this puzzle. We just have to admit that Nature is under no obligation to conform to the laws that we have evolved to further our understanding of how it functions.

The most gifted psychics who produce PK effects never have any idea how they do it. Anna Rasmussen believed that her spirit guide, Dr. Lasaruz, was responsible for hers. In more recent years Uri Geller has attributed his powers to extraterrestrial beings. But such hypotheses are at present unprovable.

In the 1970s research into PK has entered a new phase with the discovery of extraordinarily gifted subjects comparable to Anna Rasmussen and the Schneider brothers. Early research at Duke University and elsewhere suggested that PK is a faculty that many people possess in a weak form, but that cannot be developed to a spectacular degree. The comparatively recent appearances of Uri Geller and Ingo Swann have challenged this idea.

The investigations of Geller and the resulting controversies have been widely reported, but the New York artist Ingo Swann is less well known. Like Geller, he has been studied by scientists at the Stanford Research Institute in Menlo Park, California.

At the Stanford Institute, physicists Harold Puthoff and Russell Targ supervised an experiment in which Swann was required to psychokinetically disturb the inner workings of a

Below: Professor John Taylor of London University tests a child with psychokinetic ability to find a scientific explanation for such phenomenon. After appearing on a television show with Uri Geller in 1973, Taylor was convinced of the genuineness of PK powers.

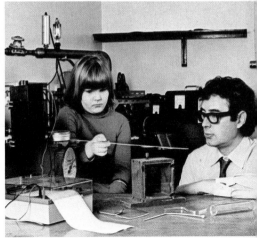

Left: Taylor tests the level of radioactivity of the child's hands—which he thinks might explain her ability to bend metal.

Above: an experiment designed by Dr. Gertrude Schmeidler of City College to discover whether PK energy generates heat. For it she used *thermistors*—temperature detectors—seen in the thermos bottles. The subject, artist Ingo Swann, was supposed to heat or cool the thermistors by PK power as directed by the experimenter.

magnetometer. This is a device that produces electric current from a radioactive core sunk deep in a well. The current decreases at a uniform rate in relation to the decay rate of the magnetic field within the instrument. The output of current is recorded in the form of a continuous wave on a moving chart. The magnetometer is shielded by special metals so that no other magnetic influences can reach it. The physicists described to Swann how the magnetometer functioned, and told him that if he could affect the magnetic field within it the change would show on the output recording. Swann then focused his attention on the interior of the magnetometer, whereupon the frequency of the output immediately doubled. In the course of the experiment he was able to cause other changes, which show up clearly on the chart. Puthoff and Targ emphasize in their report that this was not a fully controlled scientific experiment, for it left open the question whether Swann had in fact disturbed the process of subatomic emission in the radioactive core, or whether he had affected the recording device. Either way, of course, the effect he produced in the laboratory equipment could only have been produced by the operation of PK.

Dr. Gertrude Schmeidler, a professor of psychology at the City University, New York, had also conducted experiments with Swann. Starting from the question of whether PK energy generates heat, as all other forms of energy do, she designed an

Left: Dr. Gertrude Schmeidler pictured in her modern and well-equipped laboratory. Psychology is her particular field of study.

experiment using *thermistors*—extremely sensitive temperature detectors—connected to the palms of Swann's hands and also lodged in thermos bottles on the other side of a large room. The thermistors in the bottles were the targets, and Swann was instructed to employ his PK faculty to heat or cool them as directed by the experimenter. He succeeded in doing this with an effort of concentration, and Dr. Schmeidler noted that his skin temperature correspondingly decreased and increased. She also noted that a thermistor in a bottle several feet from the target cooled down when the target bottle heated up. This fact raises an interesting speculation about psychic energy. As Dr. Schmeidler put it: "Rather than Ingo transferring all of his energy to the thermistor target, it appears that he drew on energy from the environment, and when he cooled the target he transferred the energy back."

This is exactly what the earlier researcher Harry Price inferred from the thermograph records obtained during sittings with the mediums Stella Cranshaw and Rudi Schneider. Such startling physical phenomena have only rarely occurred in the parapsychological laboratory, but the combination of sophisticated modern research methods and the appearance of gifted psychics like Geller, Swann, and a few others, has enabled contemporary parapsychologists to make rapid progress toward solving the puzzle of PK.

6

Parapsychology in Eastern Europe

Josefka had been trained to exercise her psychic faculty under hypnosis. On this particular evening she was going to try an experiment in precognitive clairvoyance. Her instructions were to think of a friend and try to foresee some unpleasant event that that friend might be able to avoid if warned about it in time.

Soon after Josefka was put into trance she started to show signs of agitation. She vividly began to describe a scene involving a girl friend who lived 50 miles away. The girl was in a restaurant. A stranger approached her and they talked for a while before leaving together. "She shouldn't go,"

Everybody knows about the Soviet achievements in outer space, but fewer people know about the new directions they are pursuing in inner space—in the paranormal powers of the human mind. In the Soviet Union and other Eastern European countries, parapsychology leads in interesting new directions. Above: "eyeless sight"— the power to read with the fingers—got a great deal of attention in the Soviet Union in the 1960s. Some scientists claimed that they could teach eyeless sight to those who could see as well as to the blind. Right: possibly the most important Soviet psychic research has been Kirlian photography, which shows the aura around living organisms. Western scientists are also investigating the phenomena, among them Dr. Thelma Moss. She is shown through a Kirlian photo.

"Her description matched Josefka's trance vision in every detail"

Josefka kept saying. But in her vision her friend got on a motorcycle with the stranger and they sped away into the country. Then they stopped. "Oh my God!" Josefka cried in anguish, "He's torn her skirt." She went on to describe with mounting horror a scene of savage rape. The next day Josefka phoned her friend to tell her about the possibly precognitive nightmare she had had about her. But before she had said very much her friend interrupted. "You're too late," she said. "It's already happened—last night." Her description of what had happened to her matched Josefka's trance vision in every detail.

Josefka was one of several people who developed their psi faculty under the tutelege of Dr. Milan Ryzl, formerly of Prague, Czechoslovakia, and now resident in California. Dr. Ryzl, a biochemist turned parapsychologist, evolved a method of training people to be psychic which Dr. Leonid Vasiliev, the pioneer Russian psychical researcher, called one of the most promising developments in parapsychology. During the last few years before he left his country in 1967 Dr. Ryzl trained more than 50 volunteers to become psychic in some way. He would put a subject into an hypnotic trance and ask him, or her, to visualize certain scenes or images that he would suggest. When the subject's visualizing faculty was sufficiently evolved, Ryzl would suggest that he or she try to visualize what was happening at a particular time to a friend or relative. Some of his subjects, like Josefka, developed their capacity for clairvoyance to the point that while in trance they could psychically "drop in" on friends and see what they were doing.

It was not necessary for the trance state to be deep. Ryzl reports that Josefka once went through a whole day in a light trance and pursued her normal family and working life without

Above: Dr. Milan Ryzl, Czechoslovakian-born parapsychologist, developed a technique for training people to acquire psi powers. Ryzl, now resident in California, is one of the few researchers familiar with parapsychological work in both the East and West.

Right: Josefka, the girl who became remarkably clairvoyant under the tutelage of Dr. Ryzl.

110

anyone noticing her state of mind. She was one of the students in Ryzl's group who eventually learned to induce the trance state in themselves without the help of the hypnotist. She sometimes found it amusing, and at other times perhaps embarrassing, to pick up people's thoughts telepathically. On several occasions she found her clairvoyance useful in locating missing objects such as keys and office documents.

While he was still in Prague, Ryzl became a research associate of the Duke Parapsychology Laboratory, and in some of his work he used the ESP card-guessing tests devised by Rhine and his colleagues. In one clairvoyance experiment, for which the Zener cards were individually enclosed in thick opaque wrappings, Josefka scored 121 hits out of 250 guesses. Chance expectancy would have been 50 hits, and Josefka's performance represented odds against chance of a trillion to one. This result was obtained when she was in an hypnotic trance. In a control experiment when she was in a normal state of consciousness she scored exactly at chance level.

Ryzl's star ESP subject, a quiet-spoken man named Pavel Stepanek, quickly learned to control his psi faculty without undergoing hypnosis. Throughout the early 1960s parapsychologists from America, Britain, and The Netherlands flew to Prague to test for themselves this reputed card-guessing prodigy. The busy Dr. J. G. Pratt of Duke was among them, and after his observations he declared that "Pavel Stepanek's achievement is one that has rarely, if ever, been equaled in the history of parapsychology." The remarkable aspect of Stepanek's ESP laboratory work was that he could achieve significantly above-chance results consistently, reliably, and with any experimenter testing him. Nor did he suddenly go into decline, as all other high-scoring subjects had done. He had a short off-period in the mid-60s when for a time his scores declined to chance level and below. But when he was invited to the United States in 1967 for tests in American parapsychology laboratories, he rewarded his sponsors by achieving spectacular scores under the strictest conditions of control. He also produced a new phenomenon, which researchers called the "focusing effect." For a given card he would make the same guess repeatedly, trial after trial. The guess might be a wrong one, but it was always the same guess for such favored cards, no matter how well they were concealed in wrappings and behind screens. Apparently he was recognizing the cards but, in some cases, consistently distorting the message he received from them. Parapsychologists are still perplexed by this focusing effect. Some think that it may be a key to a breakthrough in understanding of the psi faculty, while others think it is a freak effect and a red herring.

As a research technique, hypnotism has been used much more by Eastern European and Russian researchers than by Americans and Western Europeans. It is only in recent years that systematic research into the effects of altered states of consciousness (or ASCs) on psi has been pursued in the West. This delay might be attributed to our traditional reluctance to infringe the principle of individual liberty. Relatively few Western physicians, for example, will use hypnosis in treating

Robbery by Telepathy

Even in the midst of World War II investigations into psychic phenomena went on in the Soviet Union. In one instance in 1940, the Polish psychic Wolf Messing was summoned by Stalin. The Soviet dictator had heard of Messing's telepathic power, and had a suggestion for a simple demonstration of it: Messing was to rob a bank by telepathy.

Messing chose for the experiment a big Moscow bank in which he was not known. He calmly walked in and handed the teller a blank piece of paper torn from a school notebook. He placed his case on the counter, and mentally willed the clerk to give him 100,000 roubles.

The bank clerk looked at the paper, opened the safe, and took out piles of banknotes until he had stacked 100,000 roubles on the counter. He then stuffed the money into the bag. Messing took the case, walked out of the bank, and showed the money to Stalin's two observers to prove his success as a bank robber. He then went back to the clerk and began handing the bundles of banknotes back to him. The teller looked at him, looked at the money, looked at the blank paper—and collapsed on the floor with a heart attack.

Fortunately, Messing reported, the clerk recovered.

illness. The Russians have had a different viewpoint. In the 1920s two psychologists, Professor Dzelichovski and Dr. Kotkov, ran some experiments in telepathic hypnosis with an unwitting girl student as subject. The girl had been asked to participate in some experiments with Professor Dzelichovski, but whenever she went to his laboratory for this purpose, he told her he was still waiting for some equipment to be delivered before they could begin. The girl began dropping in on the Professor on an impulse, and while she was with him chatting casually she sometimes fell asleep on her feet for a short time. She couldn't explain her behavior, but the delighted experimenters could, for both her impulsive visits and her sudden blackouts were telepathically willed on her by Dr. Kotkov. He was sitting in another room in the building, beaming his influence at her.

This story is reminiscent of the diabolical mad professor stereotype of the horror films, but we have it on no less an authority than Dr. Leonid Vasiliev, the most distinguished Russian parapsychologist and the only one whose books have been published in English translation. In his *Experiment in Mental Suggestion*, which appeared in 1962 several years before his death, Vasiliev revealed that Russian scientists had been doing research into telepathy since the 1930s. They had received orders to do so from a high authority—which suggests that Stalin may have thought that ESP would have some strategic value.

Most of these early Russian experiments were in telepathic hypnotism, and Vasiliev's accounts of them are at once fascinating and sinister. For a hypnotist to be able to knock a person out telepathically when that person is a thousand miles away, unsuspectingly conversing with someone else, is an alarming power for one human being to have over another. Yet this is what one of Vasiliev's colleagues did. He was in Sevastopol in the Crimea, and the subject, a girl, was in Leningrad. The knockout was timed to happen while the girl was with her psychiatrist, who was a party to the experiment. The Russian scientists estimate that four people in a hundred can be telepathically hypnotized at a distance, but no Western researcher has attempted to substantiate the claim.

One of Vasiliev's subjects was a woman who had been hospitalized for years suffering from psychosomatic paralysis of the

Left: Dr. L. L. Vasiliev, who was the father of Soviet parapsychology. Vasiliev's theoretical explanation for psi faculties was founded on a strictly physical basis: he said it was a remainder from earlier forms of evolution, probably operating through some kind of energy in the brain so far undiscovered.

Below: Vasiliev (second from left) with his successor Dr. Paul Gulyaiev (third from left) in the Leningrad parapsychology laboratory with other scientists.

entire left side of her body. Vasiliev, assisted by hypnotist Dr. Finne, made the woman move her paralyzed arm and leg by suggestion conveyed telepathically. They were so successful that a number of distinguished doctors went to the hospital to observe the phenomenon. First, the woman was put into trance. Then a piece of paper on which the command to be conveyed was written was passed around the group of observers. Vasiliev or Finne then concentrated mentally on the command until the woman complied with it. To rule out the possibility of her obtaining sensory cues from those present, her eyes were tightly bandaged and not a word was spoken. The degree of success was extraordinary. Finne was even able to focus on particular nerves in the paralyzed arm, and make the woman

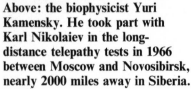

Above: the biophysicist Yuri Kamensky. He took part with Karl Nikolaiev in the long-distance telepathy tests in 1966 between Moscow and Novosibirsk, nearly 2000 miles away in Siberia.

move it in the way she would if the particular nerve that he visualized had been mechanically stimulated. The woman always knew whether it was Finne or Vasiliev who had beamed the telepathic command.

A rumor that the United States Navy was experimenting with telepathy as a means of communication with submarines led to the publication of Vasiliev's books in the Soviet Union in the early 1960s. Until then his 30 years of research work had been top secret, for telepathy posed an ideological problem for the Russians. Unless it could be shown to have a physical basis which could be explained by some kind of wave theory, it would seem to subvert the official materialist philosophy. Much of Vasiliev's early work was designed to discover the energy underlying ESP. He went to great lengths to demonstrate that it involved waves.

He put his subject inside a Faraday cage, an immense and heavy metal box which resists penetration by radio and electro-magnetic waves. Still she fell asleep when the telepathic sender, or agent, outside the cage willed her to do so. He then put the agent in a lead capsule which was sunk into a gully filled with mercury, but the girl in the Faraday cage nonetheless dropped off to order. The wave theory seemed insupportable and was quietly shelved, but the research program went on.

In 1966 a widely publicized telepathy experiment took place. The agents were in Moscow and the subject nearly 2000 miles away in Siberia. The subject was Moscow actor and journalist Karl Nikolaiev, and the agent was the biophysicist Yuri

Kamensky. Supervised by a committee of scientists, Kamensky successfully transmitted to Nikolaiev mental images of six objects which were given to him in separate packages at the start of the experiment. In another test with a different agent Nikolaiev identified 12 out of 20 ESP cards as they were turned over in Moscow.

Clairvoyance is never mentioned in accounts of Soviet ESP research, in contrast to much American work suggesting that clairvoyance may be the primary mode of ESP. Nikolaiev's feat could be attributed to clairvoyance as well as to telepathy, but the Russians are sticking to the hypothesis of a type of "mental radio" to explain such phenomena, even though they have not been able to discover the elusive radio waves. Their research has brought to light some interesting facts about brain waves, however. In a distance experiment between Moscow and Leningrad, Nikolaiev was wired up to a battery of machines that monitored his physiological changes and brain wave patterns. He put himself into a receptive frame of mind and waited. He didn't know when Kamensky, 400 miles away, was going to begin his attempt at telepathic transmission, and he had no idea what kind of message to expect. The *electroencephalograph* (brain wave recorder) registered increased activity in Nikolaiev's brain at the exact moment when Kamensky began concentrating. It also indicated that the activity took place in the part of the brain appropriate to the type of message being sent. If Kamensky sent a visual image Nikolaiev's brain was activated in the area that controls sight, and if he sent an auditory signal like a whistle the receiver's brain registered a stimulus in the area involved with sound. Referring to this research in an article in the *International Journal of Parapsychology* in 1968, Dr. Milan Ryzl said, "These Soviet findings could bring us a long way forward in the control of ESP."

Since his defection to the United States in 1967, Ryzl has served as the main source of information about psi research in the Soviet Union and Eastern Europe for Western parapsychologists and students. But his writings on the subject have all appeared in academic journals. The general public's knowledge of Eastern European parapsychology has come largely from a book entitled *Psychic Discoveries Behind the Iron Curtain* by the two young writers Sheila Ostrander and Lynn Schroeder. The authors gathered material for their book during a study-trip through the Communist countries in 1968, and published the book two years later. It was offered as a work of reportage, with the introductory caution that "Whether Communist observations and theories about psychic happenings are right or not, can only be determined by further investigations."

Despite this cautionary remark, the book gave rise to a myth that the United States and the Soviet Union are engaged in a psi-research race and that the Communists, with official backing, are forging ahead. Milan Ryzl, addressing an annual conference of the Parapsychology Foundation of New York, took a less dramatic view. He spoke of Soviet parapsychology as "cautious renaissance," and warned that, "The more spectacular ventures, which are most publicized, are more science fiction than solid pieces of scholarly study." However, he did cite a number of individual researchers and areas of investigation that he believes are contributing significantly to international progress in parapsychology. Among these important projects are Gulyaiev's research on the "electrical aura" of living bodies, Professor A. Novomeysky's investigations of "finger reading," and various studies of the PK effects produced by Mrs. Nelya Mikhailova.

Professor Ippolit Kogan designed and carried out the experiments with Nikolaiev and Kamensky. As head of the Bioinformation Unit of the A.S. Popov Society for Radiotechnics in Moscow, Kogan has completed many series of experiments in telepathy, and has also contributed to the theoretical study of the subject. He has continued Vasiliev's work on the telepathic control of consciousness using hypnotized subjects. In repeated trials, sleeping subjects have been made to wake up telepathically by an agent situated in another room. In another series of experiments with the gifted Karl Nikolaiev, Kogan's colleague Edward Naumov succeeded 13 times in 26 attempts in guiding Nikolaiev telepathically to find objects hidden in a room.

The Soviet term for telepathy, "bioinformation," indicates a bias toward finding a physical basis for the phenomenon. At one point Kogan demonstrated mathematically that if the existence of electromagnetic waves over a mile long could be assumed, telepathy might be explained in terms of this kind of radiation. Even so, the theory would not account for long-distance telepathy; and in his later theoretical work Kogan has tended toward the conclusion that telepathy can never be understood in terms of energy. Telepathy is transfer of information, and information must not be confused with energy, he maintains. Kogan illustrates his point with the example of light. To take a photograph in a dark room you need the concentrated light *energy* provided by a flashbulb. But when light conveys *information*, for instance in a warning buoy at sea, the faintest distant glimmer, requiring only minimal energy, can convey all necessary information. Bioinformation, or telepathy, Kogan suggests, may be analogous. The electromagnetic radiation of the brain is not powerful enough in terms of energy to push a message through space, but it can create a weak but detectable field of force around the body. In theory, it is possible that this field of force—or psi field—can convey information to a person who knows how to interpret the faint signal.

This theoretical model for telepathic communication relies partly on the findings of Professor Pavel Gulyaiev, Vasiliev's successor as head of the Laboratory of Physiological Cybernetics at the University of Leningrad. Using extremely sensitive apparatus specifically designed for the purpose, Gulyaiev and his colleagues have discovered that all living bodies are surrounded by a faint electrostatic field, which they call the "electrical aura." This field undergoes constant changes, and even thoughts can cause changes in it which can be detected and measured. Gulyaiev has suggested that changes in the electrical aura may represent signals which carry information, and that this may be the means by which some fish, insects, and

Above: Nelya Mikhailova with Dr. Zdenek Rejdak, one of the researchers who has worked on tests of her powers. On the table are some of the objects she had moved by PK. Dr. Rejdak strongly defended her powers as genuine.

118

Right: stills from a movie of Mrs. Mikhailova, who is also known as Madame Kulagina, moving matches on a table by PK. The observers present said that at no time did her hands come into contact with the table itself.

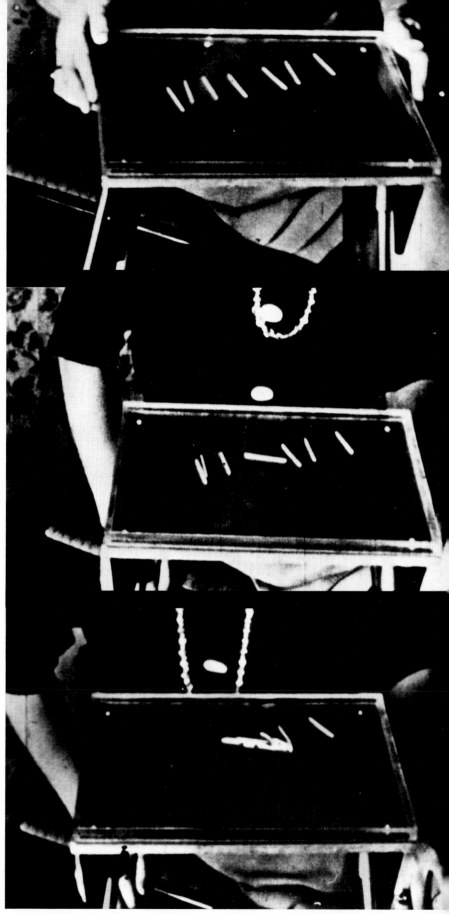

other animals communicate. It is also theoretically possible that changes in the aura, caused by mental activity, could be amplified to produce sufficient energy to move objects.

The possible connection between PK and this electrostatic field has been investigated with the cooperation of a remarkable woman, Mrs. Nelya Mikhailova. This Leningrad housewife has dazzled Soviet parapsychologists for several years with her psychokinetic powers. Among those who have tested her is Dr. Gerady Sergeyev, who designed an instrument that picks up at a distance of up to four yards the electrostatic and magnetic fields of the human body. Sergeyev's detectors showed that Nelya Mikhailova generated 50 times more voltage from the back of her head than from the front, whereas most people generate only three or four times more. This was in a normal condition of rest. When Mrs. Mikhailova was actually exercising her PK, causing small objects on a table in front of her to move, the instruments showed that the magnetic fields around her body began to pulsate, and these pulsations kept in rhythm with pulsations of her heart and brain. Moreover, she appeared to be able to focus the force-field emanating from her in the direction of the object she was looking at.

Nelya Mikhailova has been observed and reported on by a number of Western parapsychologists and writers, who all vouch for the genuineness of her effects. She can make matches, cigarettes, pens, and other light objects move on a table by moving her hands over them or just looking at them. She can tilt a pair of scales which are equally balanced with weights of 30 grams, and continue to hold one side of the scale down when 10 extra grams are added to the other side. When she stops concentrating and moves her eyes the heavier scale sinks. To accomplish these feats she often has to spend considerable time revving up her powers. When she has finished she is fatigued, and she has sometimes been found to have lost weight.

The PK talent of Nelya Mikhailova was discovered by Vasiliev in the course of investigating a different paranormal faculty she possesses: the ability to "see" with her hands. Finger-reading or eyeless sight is a predominantly Soviet area of parapsychological research. Mrs. Mikhailova is reported to have discovered her ability one day in the early 1960s when, convalescing from an illness in a Leningrad hospital, she was passing the time doing embroidery. She found that without looking she was able to pick out of the bag of thread any color that she wanted from among the many it contained. Some time later she happened to read an article about a young woman who lived in the Ural mountain city of Tagil, and who was said to be able to "see" with her fingers. Mikhailova reported her own experience to her doctor, who brought it to the attention of Vasiliev.

Rosa Kuleshova, the young woman in Tagil, really started something when she went to her doctor in 1962 and told him she had discovered that she could distinguish colors and read print with her fingers. Of course, the doctor was incredulous, but Rosa demonstrated her ability to his satisfaction, and he informed professional colleagues of the discovery. Among these was Professor Abram Novomeysky, who tested her

Above: Nelya Mikhailova trying to exert her PK powers. The odd headgear is a device to monitor her brain waves during the test.

Right: Mrs. Mikhailova is far from being the only Soviet psychic who has demonstrated PK powers in the laboratory. In these stills from a film, Alla Vinogradova is shown moving matches through PK.

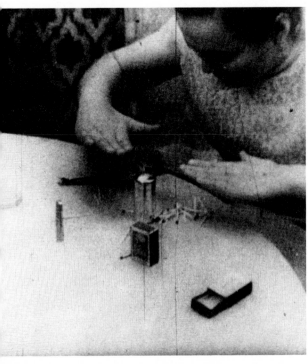

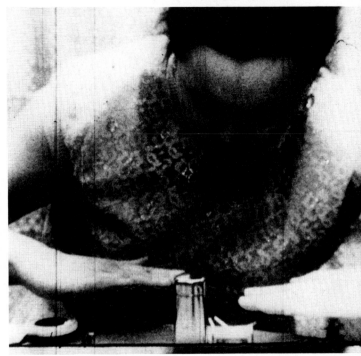

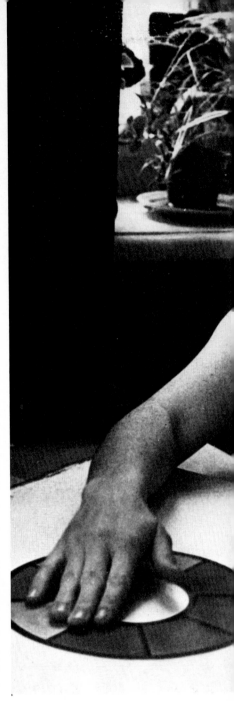

claims himself and was also satisfied that they were genuine. The provincial prodigy was then invited to demonstrate before top scientists in Moscow at the Biophysics Institute of the Soviet Academy of Sciences. After conducting their own experiments, which were carefully constructed to rule out alternative explanations such as telepathy and clairvoyance, the scientists confirmed that Rosa possessed skin sensitivity so acute that she really could "see" with her fingers.

If this were a freak phenomenon it would not be so important. But subsequent work by Professor Novomeysky and his colleagues showed that skin vision is a faculty that many people can develop. Rosa developed her ability gradually. At first she could only "see" with the fingers of her right hand, then she

Above left: Rosa Kuleshova reading a newspaper with her fingers rather than with her eyes. She caused a sensation in the Soviet Union with her psi power of seeing through the skin. This ability also extended to telling colors.

Right: even the placement of a piece of glass over the printed matter did not prevent Rosa Kuleshova from being able to read the numbers with her fingertips.

learned to do so with both hands and with other parts of her body, such as her elbow. Novomeysky found that one person in six of those he tested could learn within half an hour to tell the difference between two colors by touch. Some subjects eventually were able to distinguish all the colors, and they generally agreed on the distinctive feel of individual colors. Light blue is smooth, for example; yellow is slippery; orange is hard and rough. Subjects who actually developed the ability to distinguish colors merely by passing their hands over them found that different colors radiated their influence to different heights, as if they had a range of degrees of energy. Red appeared to extend highest and light blue the least. On the basis of this evidence Novomeysky conjectured that skin sight might be explained as an interaction between electromagnetic fields emanating both from the color and from the subject's body.

When the news of the discovery of Rosa Kuleshova and the phenomenon of eyeless sight reached the Soviet public, it caused a sensation. Many people found they possessed the faculty; others found they could simulate it; and Rosa herself, carried away by her fame, made extravagent claims that she couldn't fulfill without cheating. But in Tagil and nearby Sverdlovsk, Novomeysky and his colleagues continued studying the phenomenon using blind subjects, most of them children who had been blind from birth. By playing colored beams on the palms of the children's hands and telling them, "this is red" or "this is blue," they trained them to distinguish colors, and later to "read" print. Research work in the field was pursued in other laboratories. In Odessa Dr. Andrei Shevalev taught a blind child to "see" with the aid of a lens attached to his forehead. In Sophia, Bulgaria, Dr. Georgi Lozanov trained 60 blind children to different degrees of competence in skin vision, and demonstrated their abilities at a meeting of distinguished physicians, psychiatrists, and psychotherapists. The evidence for the reality of this paranormal faculty, or sixth sense, accumulated until it was indisputable. To cap it all, the octogenarian French novelist and physician Jules Romains pointed out in an article in the *International Journal of Parapsychology* in 1965 that he had published a study of what he called "para-optic ability" as long ago as 1920.

Of all Soviet research relating to parapsychology, however indirectly, the most publicized is the process known as Kirlian photography. Using high-frequency electrical currents, Semyon and Valentina Kirlian discovered some 30 years ago that they could obtain pictures of living organisms that showed a surrounding aura of luminescence. This aura, which is called a "bioplasmic body," may be the same force field recently detected and measured by such scientists as Gulyaiev and Sergeyev. Theorists have conjectured that all living things possess a

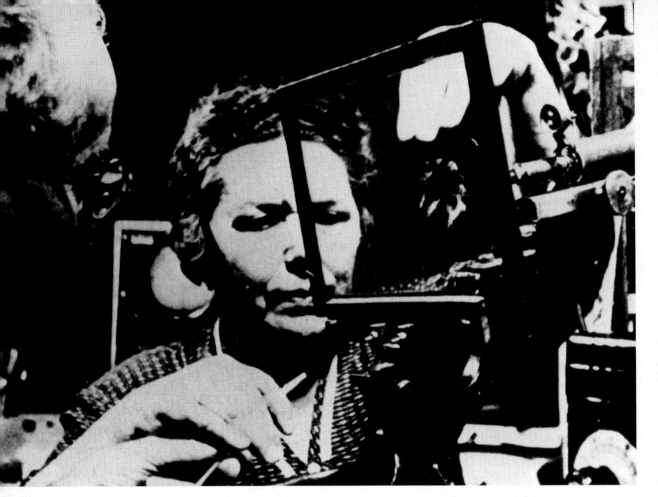

bioplasmic body. Kirlian photographs of leaves have clearly shown visible energy radiating from them, and variations in the aura of leaves of the same species have been proved to signal the onset of disease in a plant before the disease became visible by normal means. Similarly, changes in the aura of a human being may indicate changes in his mental and physical state.

Western parapsychologists have on the whole been slow to follow up the theory of a bioplasmic body, and have pointed out possible alternative explanations of the Kirlian effect. For example, Dr. Montague Ullman pointed out in an interview in *Psychic* magazine that some physicists believe the luminescence may be produced by ionization of the atmosphere. This caution on the part of Western investigators toward the bioplasma theory is understandable when one considers its resemblance to the ancient belief in an astral body coexisting with the physical body. The Kirlians' discoveries, and those of some other researchers in the Communist world, appear to support a belief generally regarded as a superstition by scientists in both the West and the East.

Nevertheless, the photographing and measuring of this force field, whatever its fundamental nature, may turn out to have important implications for parapsychology. It seems likely that this energy lies behind PK effects, and it may also play a part in psychic healing and even ESP. In the years ahead, even more exciting developments in parapsychology may emerge from laboratories in the Communist countries.

Above: Semyon and Valentina Kirlian, developers of Kirlian photography. They designed the apparatus that uses high frequency electrical currents to make visible the spectacular colored auras around all living things.

Right: this picture of the interaction between a human finger (below) and a magnet was produced by Dr. Thelma Moss, the University of California professor who has been doing a great deal of research on Kirlian photography.

124

7

Parapsychology Today

A young woman reclines at ease in a chair in a soundproof room. She can see nothing, because her eyes are covered by what looks like colored ping-pong balls cut in half. She can hear nothing, for she has on a headset through which comes only the uniform low hiss of "white noise." She is in a state of "sensory deprivation." She will remain in this state for a period of 30 minutes, and at some point during this time a friend in another room will view a series of stereoscopic slides, concentrate hard on the pictures, and try to communicate them telepathically to the young woman, who has no idea when during the 30 minutes the attempt

Some of the most interesting research in current parapsychology is in the area of sensory deprivation—isolation of the mind from stimuli. One of the goals is to see how the mind might then be influenced by ESP forces. Right: this subject is undergoing a sensory deprivation test at New York's Maimonides Hospital.

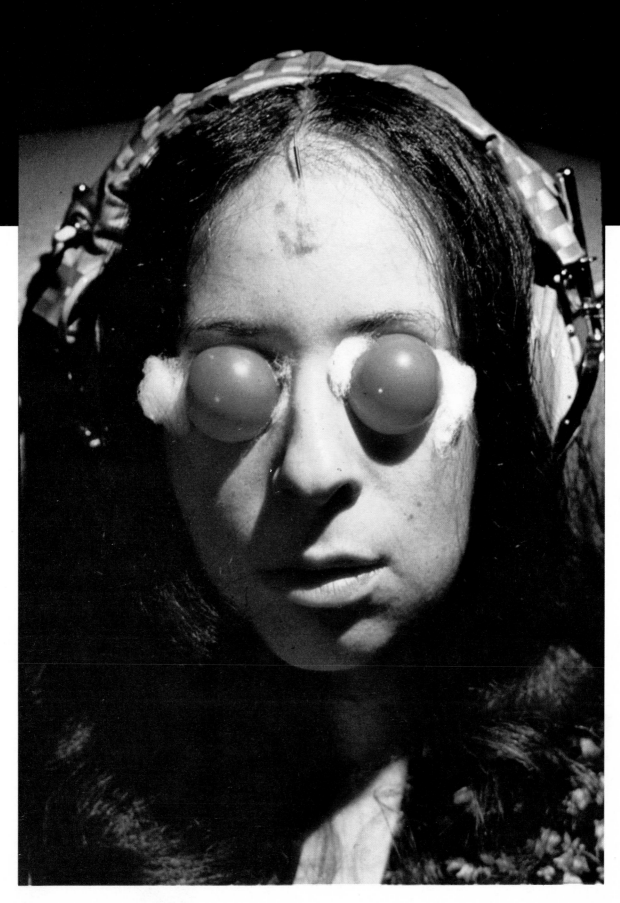

"A person will be more aware... on a purely mental level"

will take place. Throughout the entire period she gives a running commentary on what she thinks and visualizes, which is tape recorded.

This experiment was designed by Charles Honorton, director of research in the Division of Parapsychology and Psychophysics at the Maimonides Medical Center, Brooklyn, New York. It tests his theory that "conscious sensory isolation increases access to internal mentation processes." In other words, when nothing is coming in from outside by way of the senses, a person will be more aware of what is going on inside on a purely mental level. The theory also proposed that in a state of sensory deprivation a person will be more susceptible than he normally is to nonsensory influences from outside, such as telepathic communication.

In this particular experiment the theme of the target series of slides is Las Vegas. The agent views the slides, concentrating on each picture in turn, and gradually the subject's commentary begins to home in on the target. She reports that she sees bright neon lights, street scenes with a lot of activity, theater marquees.

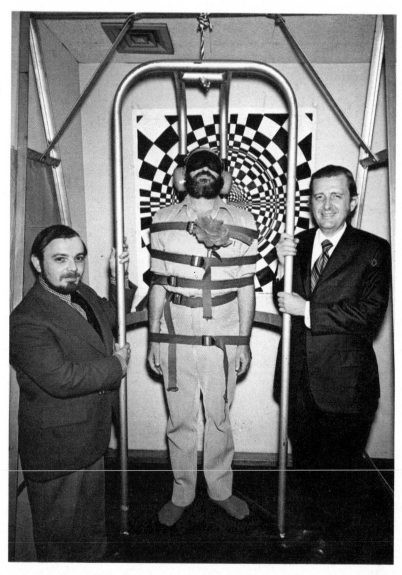

Right: Charles Honorton and Dr. Stanley Krippner flank Dr. Harry Hermon who is fastened into the witches' cradle, a device that disorients a subject spatially. Nicknamed after a trance-inducing device allegedly used by witches, it is used at Maimonides Hospital in sensory deprivation tests.

... The brightly illuminated buildings could be nightclubs. ... It could be some place such as Las Vegas. The sending period comes to an end, but the subject's continuous report on her thoughts and mental imagery continues until the prescribed time has elapsed. She is then shown four different sets of slides and asked to select one which has some correspondences with her recent stream of thought. She has no hesitation in selecting the target set, the scenes of Las Vegas. This experiment will be recorded as an unqualified hit.

Out of 27 series of such experiments, each series including 50 sessions with different subjects, Honorton reports that 20 produced a statistically significant proportion of hits. In one successful experiment the target theme of the slides viewed by the agent was "rare coins." Part of the subject's commentary during the sending period ran:" . . . now I see circles, an enormous amount of them. Their sizes are not the same . . . some are really large, and others are very tiny—no larger than a penny. They just keep flashing in front of me, all these different size circles . . . Now I see colors . . . two in particular, gold and

Below: Research in 1971 at the Maimonides Hospital centered on the "alpha state," an extremely calm state in which psi seems to be able to function best. Dr. Krippner (right) and Honorton (left) observe a sleeping subject.

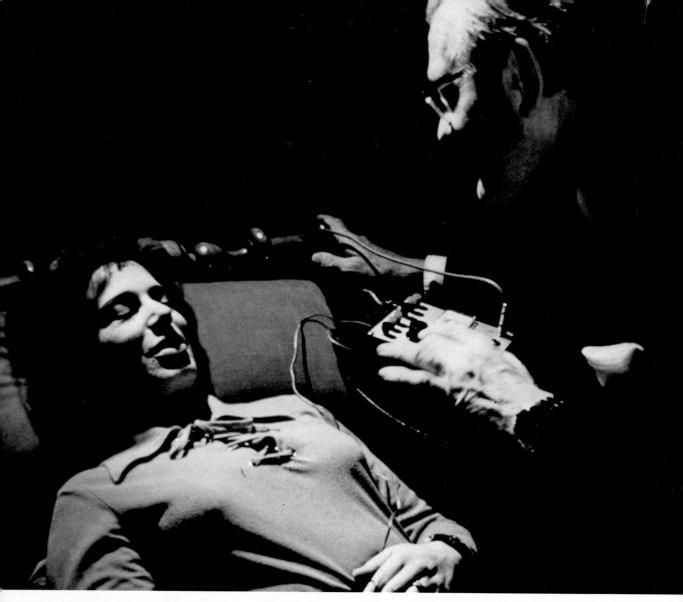

Above: Douglas Dean, shown using a *plethysmograph*, which monitors subtle variations in blood volume in any part of the body. It is used to measure a physiological reaction in a person of which he or she might be completely unaware consciously.

silver, seem to stand out more than all the others. I sense something important. I can't tell what but I get a feeling of importance, respect, value." On another occasion the target theme was "U.S. Air Force Academy," and part of the subject's commentary went: "An airplane floating over the clouds . . . planes passing overhead . . . thunder and angry clouds . . . airplanes . . . ultrasound . . . a blaze of fire, red flames . . . a giant bird flying . . . six stripes on an army uniform, V-shaped . . . the sensation of going forward very fast . . . ."

Not all the recorded hits are as unambiguous and direct as these. In assessing results, experimenters have to take into account the fact that there is not always a direct and literal correspondence between an external event and our mental reconstruction of it. For instance, on one occasion when the target pictures were taken from a news magazine story about the secret bombing of Cambodia, the subject reported images of former President Nixon cleaning his nose! Honorton doesn't say whether he counted that a hit.

This type of experiment exemplifies several characteristics of

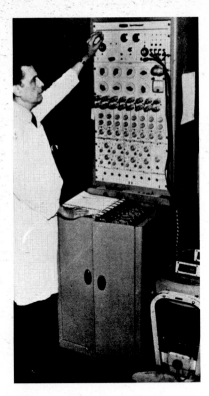

Above: Dr. Krippner monitoring an *electroencephalograph* (EEG) machine during one of the dream experiments in the special laboratory at Maimonides Hospital. In such new lines of psychical research, the approach is to discover and measure the subtle changes in the body during the exercise, or attempted exercise, of psi powers. The EEG detects electrical activity of the brain.

most of the current work in parapsychology. First, it is less concerned with proving that psi phenomena occur than with discovering under what conditions they occur and what they tell us about the properties and potentials of the human mind. Second, it doesn't necessarily revolve around work with exceptionally gifted individuals. There is a growing belief that most, if not all, people possess psi to some degree. Third, it depends less on the closed-option type of test, such as card-guessing, and gives the subject's mind freer range and more interesting challenges. Fourth, it seeks to create conditions favorable to the functioning of the psi faculty by putting the subject into an altered state of consciousness. Finally, it employs electronic and other technological aids to induce, observe, and measure psi functions.

These characteristics, taken together, constitute a revolution in parapsychology. The subject has broadened out and converged with other areas of scientific investigation and with aspects of modern social and cultural life. Perhaps, in fact, this trend in parapsychology is less a revolution than a return to origins. One of the older generation of British psychical researchers, G. N. M. Tyrrell, said in his Presidential Address to the SPR in 1945: "Let us now, before the restricted view of the laboratory worker gains too firm a hold, try to realize how wide our subject is. We should try once more to see it through the eyes of Frederic Myers as a subject which lies at the meeting place of religion, philosophy and science, whose business is to grasp all that can be grasped of the nature of human personality."

Parapsychologists today are tending to return to this broader view of their subject, and to transcend "the restricted view of the laboratory worker." Many of them believe that the traditional methods of science as adapted to parapsychological research by Rhine and his colleagues in the 1930s are self-defeating in the study of psi functions, for they inhibit their operation. They believe that the little that can be learned about psi from card guessing, dice throwing and odds-against-chance computations has already been learned, and it is time for new and more imaginative approaches. Especially talented subjects are always interesting to parapsychologists, but the best and most interesting research being done today does not involve a quest for freak superminds. It combines the broadly humanistic outlook of the founders of psychical research with the technological sophistication of the modern physicist.

Modern studies in telepathy illustrate this. The eminent Cambridge philosopher C. D. Broad pointed out that to think of telepathy as transfer of information or imagery from one mind to another is too restrictive. He preferred to speak of "telepathic interaction." This phrase suggests the idea that one mind might act upon another without their thoughts or experiences necessarily corresponding, and he suggested that telepathic interaction takes place in life more commonly than we might suppose and quite often without our noticing it. An experiment conducted by Douglas Dean of the Newark College of Engineering demonstrated Broad's concept.

Dean used a device called a *plethysmograph*, which measures

fluctuations in blood volume in any part of the body. The index finger of the subject was connected to this device. In another room the agent was given a list of names and instructed to concentrate on the names one at a time in random order, making a note of the time at which he concentrated on each name. At the same time he was to visualize the subject and his location. Some of the names were of people listed in a telephone directory, but others were of people emotionally connected to the subject, such as his wife, his mother, or his child. Now when a person receives information that has emotional significance for him, his body may react in certain ways including change in blood pressure. In this experiment the plethysmograph frequently registered significant changes in the subject's blood volume when the agent concentrated on names of people the subject was close to. But when the agent was thinking about an unfamiliar name there were no such changes. The significant point of this experiment is that the subject was never *consciously* aware of what the agent was thinking. He never said, for instance, "Now he's thinking of Mary, my wife." Without the plethysmograph, nobody would have known that a telepathic interaction was taking place. In Dean's experiments about one person out of four showed a measurable response to telepathic messages of emotional content. The implication would seem to be that many of us may be physiologically reacting to other people's thoughts, even though we may not be able consciously to formulate the impressions they are making on us.

The dream telepathy experiments of Dr. Montague Ullman and Dr. Stanley Krippner at the Maimonides Hospital are perhaps the best-known modern investigations of telepathy. They have established clearly that telepathic communication is neither a rare occurrence confined mainly to times of crisis nor a special aptitude possessed by a few rare individuals.

The subject of Ullman and Krippner's experiments were ordinary people who volunteered to spend a night at the dream laboratory wired to an EEG (electroencephalograph) and to report on their dreams when they were awakened. It had been found that when a person is dreaming his eye make rapid movements beneath the closed lids. The EEG monitored these movements and enabled the experimenter, in another room, to see when the subject was dreaming, and to awaken him to obtain a report on his dream while it was still vivid to him. In yet

another room in the laboratory sat the agent. At the beginning of the session he selected an envelope from a group of 12, using a special method to insure a random choice. Each of the envelopes contained a postcard reproduction of a painting. The agent had to concentrate on this picture throughout the night and attempt to transmit his impressions of it to the sleeping subject. In the morning the tapes of the subject's dream reports and the target picture were given to independent judges who assessed the dreams for their correspondence, if any, to the target picture.

What emerged strongly from hundreds of such experiments— and from the many spontaneous cases of dream telepathy collected by Ullman and Krippner—is that telepathic communication to a sleeping subject is a fairly frequent occurrence. However, the process is more of an infiltration of the dreamer's consciousness than a complete invasion of it. The target picture was never transmitted whole, as an image, but was broken up, and elements from it were interwoven with the sleeper's ongoing dream. Sometimes these elements were translated by the dreamer into an analogous form, just as in dreams we normally express material from real life in symbolic forms. For instance, one target picture was of two dogs standing with bared teeth over a piece of meat. The subject dreamed that she was at a dinner party with several other people, among them two friends who were noted for their greed and concern that others shouldn't get more than they did, especially of meat—"because in Israel,"

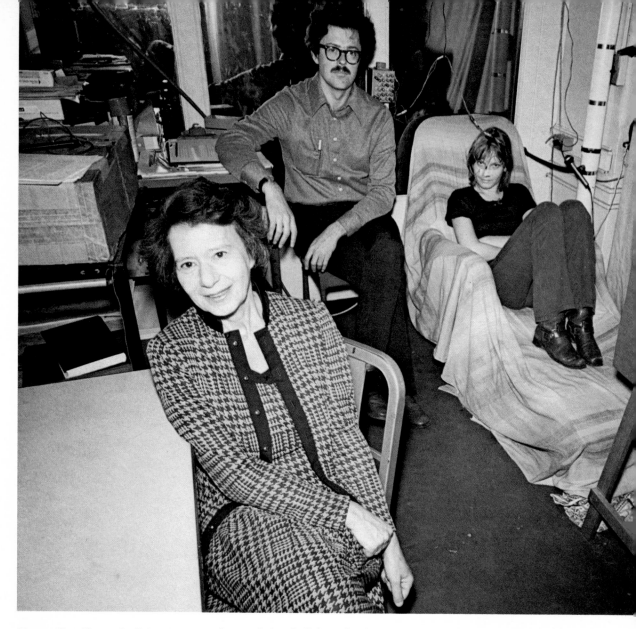

she explained, "they don't have so much meat." She was eating
"something like rib steak" and was very aware of her friends
eyeing her plate. There were no dogs in her dream, but it clearly
incorporated the themes of greed and the eating of meat that
were in the target picture.

A more literal correspondence was obtained with a picture
showing a group of Mexican revolutionaries riding against a
background of mountains and dark clouds. Part of the sleeper's
account of his first dream of the night went: "A storm. Rainstorm. It reminds me of traveling . . . approaching a rainstorm,
thunder cloud, rainy . . . a very distant scene . . . For some
reason, I got a feeling, now, of New Mexico when I lived there.
There are a lot of mountains around New Mexico. Indians,
Pueblos. Now my thoughts go to almost as though I were thinking of another civilization."

This is pretty well a direct hit, and there are many others
given in Ullman, Krippner, and Vaughan's book *Dream
Telepathy*, which gives a detailed account of the work of the

Above: target picture used by Dr. Betty Humphrey in a test relating ESP and personality factors. Below: a clairvoyant reproduction as drawn by an "expansive" person—the type that has been shown to score better in most ESP tests. Bottom: the same target picture drawn clairvoyantly by a "compressive" person. Such people are less likely to have psi ability.

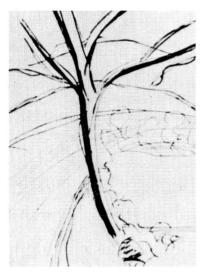

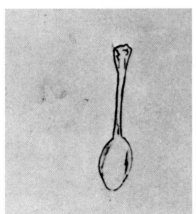

Maimonides Dream Laboratory team. Research such as this, along with Dean's work with the plethysmograph, has corroborated Professor Broad's idea that telepathy may not be a paranormal phenomenen at all but rather a feature of everyday life which generally goes unrecognized.

So perhaps all of us are psychic. This is one of the conclusions that contemporary parapsychologists are reaching. Clearly, however, some are more psychic than others, and another major area of present day research is into the conditions and personality factors that favor psi functions.

The pioneer of this type of research is Dr. Gertrude Schmeidler of the City University of New York. In the late 1940s and early 1950s Dr. Schmeidler conducted thousands of clairvoyance experiments with standard Zener cards, asking each subject before the test began whether he or she believed that ESP was possible under the conditions of the experiment. The purpose of the question was to "separate the sheep from the goats." Believers in the possibility of ESP were called sheep and disbelievers goats. Analysis of thousands of runs showed that sheep consistently scored slightly above chance, while goats scored slightly below it. Belief in success appeared to have a positive influence on scoring, and disbelief a negative influence. Dr. Schmeidler also discovered that the difference between the two groups was sharpened by making the experimental conditions pleasanter for the sheep than for the goats.

Another early researcher into the effect of personality factors was Dr. Betty Humphrey of the Duke Parapsychology Laboratory. Before administering an ESP test she asked the subject to draw anything he wished on a blank sheet of paper. This is a standard psychological test. People who produce bold, uninhibited drawings using all available space are categorized as "expansive" types, and those who produce drawings that are small, timid, or conventional are categorized as "compressive." The terms correspond more or less to the more common ones of "extravert" and "introvert." Dr. Humphrey found that her expansive subjects consistently scored positively in standard ESP tests, whereas the compressives tended to score below chance.

Dr. Margaret Anderson and Rhea White carried research into the classroom in order to study the effect of interpersonal relations on psi functioning. They found that the highest scores were turned in by pupils who liked and were liked by the teacher who administered the test. Approximately chance results were obtained when the teacher-pupil relationship involved no particular feeling on either side, and significantly below chance results were obtained when the pupil and teacher positively disliked each other.

These relatively simple pioneer experiments of the 1940s and 1950s established that personality factors and interpersonal relationships affect psi functioning. A great deal more research has been and is still being done in this area, and it has become increasingly sophisticated.

All the experiments described so far were with subjects in normal states of consciousness. The next logical step after examining the factors that encourage psi in normal states was to

Above: two researchers connected with the American Society for Psychical Research watch the read-out on a polygraph machine during an experiment. The subjects, in another room, are trying to achieve an alpha state. Above right: the subjects in the experiment. Their aim is to reach a state in which their brain transmits alpha waves. The electrodes fixed to their heads send their brain waves to the control room's polygraph machine.

find out whether deliberately induced alterations in states of consciousness would amplify the psi faculty. Rhine, in his early work at Duke, had discovered that the depressant drug sodium amytal adversely affects the psi faculty, and that the stimulant caffeine restores it to a normal level. Dr. Schmeidler went into hospitals and discovered that in the passive states of mind following concussion or childbirth psi functioning was significantly enhanced. Evidence from the fields of religion and anthropology, as well as early psychical research with mediums, testified to the fact that the trance state is conducive to psi. Now, with the development of the EEG and other electronic aids, it has become possible for a person after a little training to induce, at will, a state of mind favorable to psi.

The psi faculty has always been thought to be elusive and uncontrollable, but a new medical technique called "biofeedback" may succeed in bringing it under control. The principle of biofeedback is that a person who is provided with immediate knowledge of his internal body processes can learn to control some that normally operate involuntarily. In a typical biofeedback session a subject sits comfortably in a chair with electrodes attached to the back of the head, right forearm, and two fingers of the right hand. He wears a special jacket equipped with a respiration gauge. He aims to self-regulate muscle tension, body temperature, and brain wave rhythm. The electrodes detect changes in these internal states and relay the information back to the subject by means of three bars of light on a screen in front of him. The bars, like that of a mercury thermometer, become taller or shorter in response to changes in the physiological state that each is monitoring.

The subject first aims to achieve complete relaxation, and can watch the progress of this effort on the feedback meter wired to the muscle in his forearm. Having achieved this, he concentrates on raising temperature, while the electrodes attached to his fingers measure his success and relay the information to the second bar on the screen. He then tries to induce an extremely calm yet alert state of consciousness that is characterized by

distinctive patterns of brain activity called alpha rhythms. When the subject manages to produce alpha rhythms for a period of 10 seconds the third bar on the screen rises to its maximum height.

An alpha state has been found to be the state of consciousness most favorable to psi functioning. In 1971 Charles Honorton ran a significant experiment with subjects who had been trained to put themselves into an alpha state. It was a straightforward clairvoyance card test, but each subject was required to go through two series of guesses. For the first series, the subject lay in a semidark room with his eyes closed, and made his guesses when the EEG indicated that he was in an alpha state. For the second series he sat with open eyes under bright light—conditions which inhibit the production of alpha rhythms. The results showed a consistent and highly significant difference between the scores attained under the different conditions, and demonstrated that the alpha state of profound calm combined with alertness is especially favorable for the occurrence of psi.

Dr. Elmer Green of the Menninger Foundation in Topeka, Kansas, is an expert on biofeedback and voluntary control of internal states. He has conducted experiments with two masters of mind–body control, the Indian yogi Swami Rama, and the American mystic Jack Schwarz. Swami Rama demonstrated control of the arteries in his wrist by simultaneously warming up one spot on the palm of his hand and cooling another spot only two inches away until there was a difference of 9°F between them. He slowed down his heartbeats from 70 a minute to 52, taking less than a minute to effect the change. Then, for the sake of the experiment and to demonstrate what yogic training could achieve, he offered to stop his heartbeat completely for three or four minutes. Dr. Green said that an arrest of 10 seconds would be enough to prove his point, and the Swami promptly obliged, but extended the period to 17 seconds. This made some of the observers start to panic. He also demonstrated what he called "yogic sleep." He went into a deep sleep, snoring gently, and the EEG showed heavy delta waves that are characteristic of a

Above: biofeedback moves into the commercial field through a group called Silva Mind Control, an American organization which conducts sessions leading to "functioning in the alpha." This is a group of Silva graduates.

Above: as part of biofeedback tests, Dr. Elmer Green of the Menninger Foundation prepares the well-known Indian yogi Swami Rama for a test in which he will record his brain waves. He hopes to determine how the Swami exerts control over his normal physical reactions.

mental state of total oblivion to the world. Every five minutes a laboratory assistant made a statement in a very low voice. When the prearranged period of 25 minutes had elapsed, Swami Rama promptly sat up and repeated word for word every statement that the assistant had made. It was as if he had been deeply asleep and wide awake at the same time.

Jack Schwarz, says Green, is "one of the greatest talents in the country and probably the world in the realm of voluntary bodily controls." In his early teens he was drawn to Eastern philosophy and began to practice meditation regularly. He taught himself to perform many of the feats attributed to Hindu and Muslim fakirs. At the age of 16 he was able to lie on a bed of sharp nails and to allow a man to stand on his stomach while he was doing so. At Green's laboratory he demonstrated his powers of pain control by allowing burning cigarettes to be held against his forearm, and by driving a knitting needle through his biceps. When the needle was removed a little blood appeared, but Schwarz said, "Now it stops," and the bleeding immediately stopped. While he was performing these and similar feats, the EEG recorded a steady production of alpha rhythms.

According to Green, both Swami Rama and Jack Schwarz are able to report correctly on the past, present, and future conditions, both physical and mental, of people they do not know and have never seen. Schwarz claims also to be able to read people's auras. He amazed a visiting psychiatrist at the Menninger

Left: yoga has traditionally been a method by which students gain conscious control of their involuntary actions. The techniques of Eastern meditation are now being scientifically measured and investigated in many prominent Western laboratories.

Foundation by giving a detailed account of the doctor's own medical history and condition.

Anyone, says Schwarz, can do what he does. It is a matter of training and practice. Today, with the EEG and biofeedback techniques, the training can be greatly speeded up. Some years ago the so-called autonomic physiological systems, which include blood flow, temperature, and brain waves, were thought to be inaccessible to control by the will, but today students can learn to regulate them after just a few training sessions. There are indications that psi faculties may also be brought under control by similar methods.

A man who has developed psychic faculties in himself and others without using the biofeedback method is the New York psychologist Lawrence LeShan. In an important recent book *The Medium, the Mystic and the Physicist,* LeShan describes how he made himself a psychic healer. His training as an experimental psychologist predisposed him to believe that the alleged evidence for the paranormal "must be due to bad experimental design, false memories, hysteria, and chicanery." On the other hand, he thought that if the evidence were valid it could be of tremendous importance for science and life, and he decided to try to discover the truth for himself. He remembered that the great French chemist Lavoisier had stated authoritatively that meteorites were an impossible fable because it was obvious that there were no stones in the sky, and LeShan didn't want to risk commiting a similar error by dismissing psi as impossible just because it didn't fit in with prevailing scientific ideas of reality.

LeShan started his independent inquiry by investigating the evidence provided by sensitives. (The term "sensitive" is generally used instead of "medium" today because it doesn't suggest an intermediary between the world of the living and the spirits of the dead.) He was fortunate in that one of the most gifted, serious, and respected sensitives of modern times, the late Eileen Garrett, was then living in New York and willing to cooperate with him. He spent more than 500 hours questioning Eileen Garrett and designed several experiments in which she willingly participated. On one occasion when Mrs. Garrett was in Florida and LeShan was going to join her the following day, he prepared an experiment in psychometry in advance. While in his office in New York, he collected several different objects including an old Greek coin, a woman's comb, a fossil fish, a bit of stone from Mt. Vesuvius, a scrap of bandage, and an ancient Babylonian clay tablet. He wrapped each object in tissue, sealed it in a small box, and put the box into a manila envelope. Another person put the envelopes, which were numbered, into larger envelopes marked with different numbers. This person had the list of both code numbers but did not know which objects were in which envelopes. Thus, no one, including LeShan, could convey any information about the content of any envelope to Eileen Garrett. Mrs. Garrett was to be given the envelopes in turn and would attempt to describe details of the history of the object it contained.

While assembling the materials LeShan found that he needed another box, so he went to a neighboring office and asked a secretary, whom he only knew by sight, if she could provide one. The secretary went into his office to find out what size of box would be needed, and in the course of their conversation she picked up and examined the clay tablet. A suitable box was found in LeShan's own office, and he forgot the whole small incident. Two weeks later and 1500 miles away, LeShan and Eileen Garrett tried the psychometry experiment. She picked up an envelope— later found to contain the clay tablet—and immediately said there was "a woman associated with this." She described the secretary in such detail, LeShan says, that it would have been possible to pick her out of a line-up of 10,000 women. She even mentioned two scars that proved to be there.

Such evidence as this convinced LeShan of the reality of paranormal faculties. After examining the testimony of Eileen Garrett and other sensitives, as well as the writings of the great mystics and some modern physicists, he formulated a theory that two distinct orders of reality exist. One he called "Sensory Reality" and the other "Clairvoyant Reality." Paranormal faculties develop, he says, when a person moves out of the Sensory and into the Clairvoyant Reality. The difference between the two is largely a difference of thought and attitude, of ways of looking at the world. Most of us live most of the time on the level of Sensory Reality, basing our thoughts on the information conveyed through our senses. We see people and things as separate entities, and we consider the most important things about them to be the properties that make them individual. From the other point of view, that of Clairvoyant Reality, the important thing

Below: Lawrence LeShan, who set up the experiments with medium Eileen Garrett in an independent investigation into the powers of sensitives. He also taught himself to be a psychic healer, mainly by using techniques of meditation.

Left: Mrs. Eileen J. Garrett, one of the most famous mediums of the 20th century. Interested in trying to understand her own psychic gifts, she cooperated fully with LeShan and other psychical researchers who tested her.

about an individual is her relationship to the rest of the universe. All beings—and even inanimate substances like rock, water, and earth—are seen as parts of a whole. Time, also, is perceived differently; it does not necessarily flow in one direction at an even pace. Our everyday concepts of past, present and future are seen as illusions.

In distinguishing and describing these two kinds of reality, LeShan quotes several modern physicists. The atomic physicist J. Robert Oppenheimer, for example, acknowledged the existence of two realities in these words: "These two ways of thinking, the way of time and history and the way of eternity and timelessness, are both parts of man's efforts to comprehend the world in which he lives. Neither is comprehended in the other nor reducible to it. They are, as we have learned to say in physics, complementary views, each supplementing the other, neither telling the whole story."

Having provisionally accepted the existence of a separate plane of reality in which psi is possible, LeShan wanted to test this theory with reference to a particular aspect of psi. He chose psychic healing as his area of study. After reading the available literature on the subject and observing and talking with a number of healers, he came to the conclusion that there are two basic types of psychic healing. In Type 1 the healer goes into an altered state of consciousness in which he views himself and the patient as one. He doesn't touch the patient, or attempt to do anything; he just concentrates on a sense of being at one with the patient and with the universe, and on deep intense caring. In Type 2 the healer tries to heal, to turn on a flow of energy. He lays his hands on the patient's body on either side of the affected area, and often the patient remarks that he feels heat in that part of his body.

LeShan then began to train himself to achieve the state of consciousness required for Type 1 healing. His goal was to attain awareness of Clairvoyant Reality and in that state to become one with the patient for a few moments. His training consisted of learning to meditate. After a period of a year and a half, he learned to achieve a state of mind in which he could heal.

His attempts were not always successful. He also points out that when healing did take place, it might in some cases be due to other causes. Yet in many cases the positive biological changes that occurred seemed almost certainly due to the healing encounter. Sometimes he supplemented the Type 1 approach with a Type 2 laying on of hands, frequently with successful results.

As a scientist LeShan couldn't accept a successful experiment as valid unless it was repeatable. It was possible, he suggested, that he had been a natural psychic healer all along without realizing it. If the technique he had developed was the cause of his success, then it should work for others, he reasoned.

It does. Since 1970 LeShan has been holding training seminars for groups of psychologists and students, and many acts of healing have been carried out by these people in the course of the work. Various side-effects have been noticed, particularly intense telepathic communication between members of the groups and between healer and patient.

Le Shan's work is characteristic of some of the best being done in the area of parapsychology today, for it does not aim primarily to prove the existence of the psi faculties but rather to explore and develop them and to bring them into operation in daily life. It demands a degree of personal commitment and a shift of theoretical viewpoint that perhaps few orthodox scientists would be capable of. In the last analysis, however, such work is a genuine contribution to science, for it is bringing what was thought to be unknowable and unpredictable into the realm of the known and the controllable. It suggests that what today we call paranormal we may in the not too distant future regard as entirely normal.

The early psychical researchers asked, "Is there life after death?" Today's parapsychologists are asking, "Are there latent faculties in man that can be developed to enhance life *before* death?" And that is a revolution.

143

Picture Credits